STRETCHING YOUR LEARNING EDGES:

GROWING (UP) AT WORK

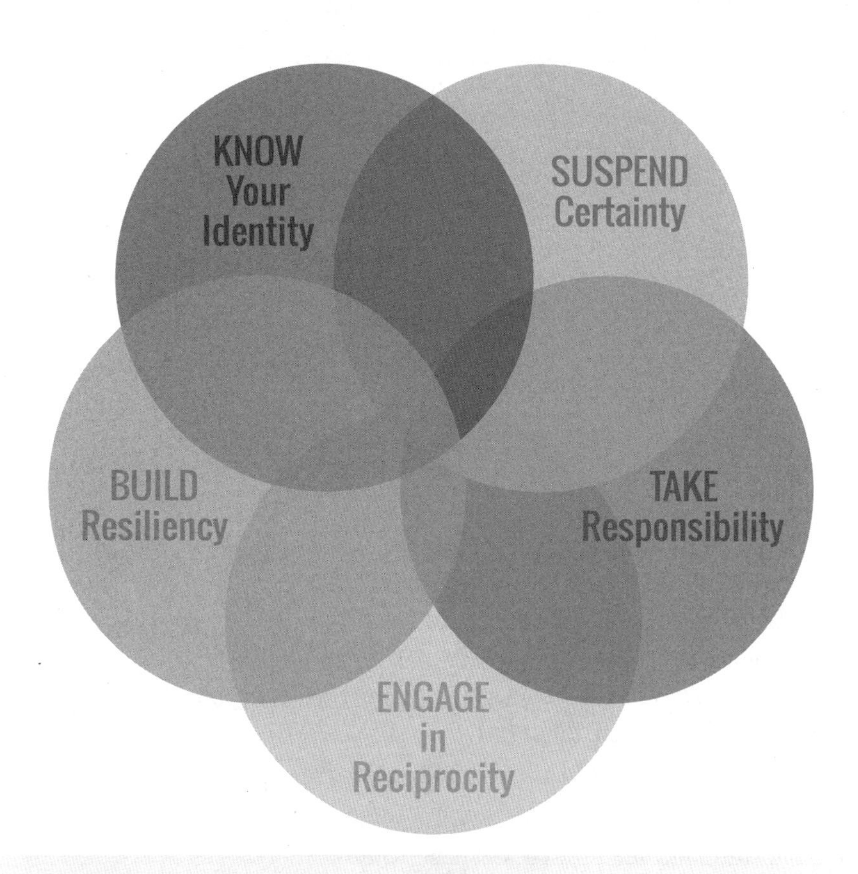

JENNIFER ABRAMS

MiraVia, LLC, Burlington, VT

Follow us @MiraViaP

STRETCHING YOUR LEARNING EDGES:

GROWING (UP) AT WORK

JENNIFER ABRAMS

PERMISSIONS

Bregman, Peter. *13 Ways We Justify, Rationalize, or Ignore Negative Feedback.* Harvard Business Review, February 14, 2019. https://hbr.org/2019/02/13-ways-we-justify-rationalize-or-ignore-negative-feedback

National School Reform Faculty, Harmony Education Center. *NRSF Protocols and Activities . . . From A to Z: The Final Word.* https://www.nsrfharmony.org/wp-content/uploads/2017/10/final_word_0.pdf

Lazare, Aaron. *On Apology.* Oxford: Oxford University Press, 2004.

Thinking Collaborative. *Adaptive Schools Resources: Norms of Collaboration, Annotated Norms.* www.thinkingcollaborative.com/as-resources

10 9 8 7 6 5 4 3 2 1

Printed in the United States of America

ISBN 978-0-9981770-3-8 Softcover

MiraVia, LLC
www.miravia.com

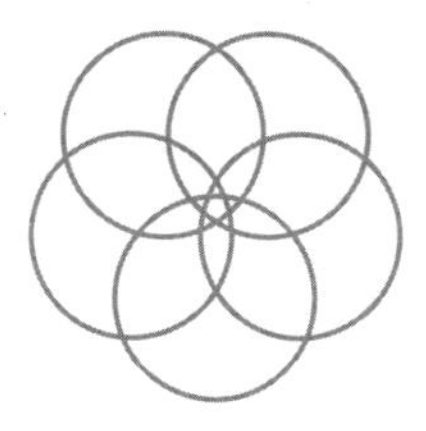

*I dedicate this book to my nephews, Joe and Evan Abrams.
As they continue on their developmental journey through
childhood, into their adolescence, and beyond,
may they be surrounded by awake, kind, and
constantly developing adults.*

Acknowledgments

- To my friends who are part of my extreme self-care support team. John Hebert, John Fredrich, Stewart Levine, Francisco Rojano-Vasquez, Stephanie Brown, Sharon Ofek, Ann Idzik, Jen Wakefield, Jason Rodriguez, Nathan Corrick, Sally Barlow-Perez, and Jane Kise. They provided me with an ear, a hug, many good dinners, several kicks in the butt, mail pickups, a great Facebook post now and then, a text of support, memories of sunrises and sunsets, and a place to just be me — however emotionally underdeveloped I felt I was. I am always grateful.

- To my colleagues who invited me in, shared their stories with me, and helped me see the challenges of supporting adult development firsthand. Angela Orr and Nicolette Smith at Doral Academy of Northern Nevada. Katy Bimpson at Juana Briones Elementary (Palo Alto, CA). Keri Shimimoto and her colleagues at the Hawaii Department of Education. And so many others. Because adult development is so important at this time worldwide, to those I have met in my work a bit farther away from home: Graham Watts, Michael Boots, Chris Charleson, Arnie Bieber, Jacques Perche, Kevin Ruth, Beth Dressler, Martha Perry, Liz Gale, Nicola Davidson, Kristen Dickhaut, and Shaz Bailley. There are also piles of gratitude for Danny Sunshine Bauer, Shirley Tokheim, and Ann Lorey. To my book concepts interviewees extraordinaire: Angeline Aow, Melissa Schaub, Cathy Gassenheimer, Heather Lageman, Kristin Moreland, Teresa Shockley, Juanita Henry, Pat Mulliken, Lauri Heffernan, Barb Novak, and Libby Bonesteel. And of course, my Warriors for the Human Spirit study group buddies, Celia Young and Monica Brinkerhoff; trio buddies from my Conversations at the Growing Edge group, Larry Ledgerwood and Patti Cotton; and those in my Leading Inclusively cohort and Ubuntu Group. All of you loved me as I stretched at my edges. Thank you.

- Finally, loads of appreciation and respect for Laura Lipton and Bruce Wellman, who asked me to publish with them and invited me on this development journey with open hearts, keen minds, and lots of support. I will be ever grateful for the invitation to work and develop with their friendship, guidance, and leadership.

  Onward!

Our conversations invent us. Through our speech and our silence, we become smaller or larger selves. Through our speech and our silence, we diminish or enhance the other person, and we narrow or expand the possibilities between us. How we use our voice determines the quality of our relationships, who we are in the world, and what the world can be and might become. Clearly, a lot is at stake here.

—Harriet Lerner, *The Dance of Connection*

Contents

Videos & Exercises

EXERCISES

EXERCISES

About the Author

Jennifer Abrams is an international education and communications consultant for public and independent schools, hospitals, universities, and nonprofits. During her twenty-six-year tenure at Palo Alto Unified School District in California, Jennifer led professional development sessions on topics from equity and elements of effective instruction to teacher leadership and peer coaching, and she facilitated teacher and administrator workshops at both the elementary and secondary levels. From 2000–2011 Jennifer was lead coach for the Palo Alto-Mountain View-Los Altos-Saratoga-Los Gatos Consortium's Beginning Teacher Support and Assessment Program. Jennifer trains and coaches teachers, administrators, nurses, hospital personnel, and others on new employee support, supervision, being generationally savvy, having hard conversations, and collaboration skills.

In her educational consulting work, Jennifer has presented at annual conferences, including Learning Forward, Association for Supervision and Curriculum Development, National Association of Secondary School Principals, National Association of Elementary School Principals, and the New Teacher Center Annual Symposium, as well as at the Principal's Training Center and Teacher's Training Center for International Schools. Internationally, Jennifer has been invited to present at EARCOS, NESA, TAISI, ECIS, AISA, AASSA, CEESA and Tri-Association conferences and at schools across Asia, Europe, Australia and New Zealand, as well as in South America and Canada. Education Week's blog, *Finding Common Ground,* recognized Jennifer as one of twenty-one women all K–12 educators need to know, and the International Academy of Educational Entrepreneurship has named her an entrepreneur of the year. She has also been a featured interviewee on the topic of professionalism for ASCD's video series, *Master Class,* hosted by National Public Radio's Claudio Sanchez.

Jennifer's publications include *Having Hard Conversations*; *The Multigenerational Workplace: Communicate, Collaborate, and Create Community*; *Hard Conversations Unpacked: The Whos, the Whens, and the What-ifs*; and *Swimming in the Deep End: Four Foundational Skills for Leading Successful School Initiatives.* Jennifer writes a monthly newsletter blog, *Voice Lessons,* available at www.jenniferabrams.com. To learn more about Jennifer's work, visit www.jenniferabrams.com and follow her @jenniferabrams on Twitter.

PREFACE

Where Did This Book Come From and How Do I Read It?

Like many Jewish teenagers, I had a bat mitzvah when I was thirteen. According to Jewish tradition, the ceremony marks the point of transition to adulthood in the Jewish community. For several months prior to the occasion, I memorized lines and lines of Torah, wrote a few speeches, and learned how to write thank-you notes. In Jewish culture, I became an adult at thirteen. I was accountable for my actions. For me, my adult life also began because I started wearing pantyhose.

My father spoke to me on the bema the day of my bat mitzvah and told me how proud he was of me. He then said he wished for me to move forward into adulthood by living the words from Micah 6:8: "To act justly, to love mercy, and to walk humbly with your God." This hope was a lot to take in. I was just learning how to write a proper thank-you note and how not to run my nylons! These strong recommendations from my father were overwhelming. I hadn't even gotten my braces yet.

Fast forward. Five years later I graduated from high school, and then four years after that I completed university. I flew to San Francisco from Boston and worked at a summer school within six weeks of receiving my college diploma. And to make matters even more adult, I had a position for the fall with one period student teaching and one period as a teaching intern. As an intern, I was the teacher of record for twenty-five tenth graders, all about fifteen years old. At the time, I was twenty-two years old, only seven years their senior.

Looking back, I realize that I was just growing up myself. Graduating from undergrad, becoming teacher of record, and being responsible for the education of a group of teenagers is a lot of adulting behavior in one gulp. In the United States, it's not uncommon in many schools to have teachers in their early twenties teach students in their teens. And so, there I was being the grown-up in the room.

After ten years teaching high-school English, I began work as a new teacher coach, inducting new teachers into the profession. As a mentor, I helped others navigate the world of education and learn the norms around what it means to be a professional and an educator.

I discovered quickly that I had a credential to teach students the subject of English, but I didn't have a credential in how talk effectively to adults or in how to be a professional.

I discovered quickly that my credential in teaching students English did not cover how to speak effectively to adults, how to work effectively as a group member or how to be a professional. The next decade and a half was spent working with new teachers in a school district and brought me an ever clearer awareness that while new teacher support focused on what happens in the classroom, what happens outside the classroom—in meetings, in teams, in adult-to-adult discussions—was just as essential to the work of education. Yes, one could learn how to coach, supervise, facilitate, and support colleagues; many of us took courses on these topics and read countless books about these skills. Yet not all of us actually learned these critical skills—those skills learned directly from working with adults day to day. Yet, knowing how to be our best selves and modeling what it means to be an emotionally self-regulated, mature, and respectful colleague is important for all of us whether we are in meetings with adults daily or only a few times a week. Plus, it is important for our students and for the communities in which we serve. Research backs up that adults who collaborate effectively and trust in one another are essential to productivity and student learning, but even more important is how, without saying a word, we teach students through the example of our interactions with one another. In schools, students are always watching.

I left my former school district after twenty-six years, and I developed an independent communications consulting business. I have written books and moved into the role of facilitator, author, and speaker. Through it all, the idea of adult development—not just what it means to be a professional, but how to become a more developed human being—is never far from my mind.

My books about having hard conversations, collaborating effectively across generations, and successfully rolling out school initiatives all center around my belief that interactions in the workplace need to be humane and growth producing. What I first assumed, then questioned, and now try to articulate, is that there exists a foundational set of professional skills, capacities, and mindsets, and there is a way to develop beyond a baseline—beyond an introductory level of how to get along at work. We have an opportunity to stretch. We can develop with intent. We can *learn* to grow up.

As I was writing my most recent book, my father was diagnosed with cancer and passed away six months later. I am now the elder in my immediate family—the big sister, the aunt. The high bar he set for me 40 years ago remains at the forefront of my work: Who am I? Who do I want to be? Am I my best self? How do I live out the values my father mentioned in his speech so many years ago as I moved into my adulthood?

This continued quest to define what it means to grow up and develop into a more aware, thoughtful, responsible, empathic, broad-minded, and resilient person strongly aligns with my work over the two plus decades to support adults in schools. This quest leads me to ask: How can we stretch ourselves at our learning edges? What does it mean to grow (up)?

DEFINITIONS

grown-up *adj.*
- having reached the age of maturity; not childish
- characteristic of adults: grown-up behavior

noun.
- a person who has reached the age of maturity; adult

professional *adj.*
- participating in an occupation as a means of livelihood or for gain
- of or relating to a profession
- appropriate to a profession
- engaged in a learned profession

noun.
- someone who is professional

adult *adj.*
- grown-up; mature
- of or relating to adults
- intended for adults; not suitable for children

noun.
- a person who is fully grown
- a person who is age of maturity as specified by law

level up (informal) *verb.*
- progress to the next level
- advance one's character to the next level of development

step up *verb.*
- increase, augment, or advance, especially by one or more steps
- come forward to claim responsibility
- succeed in meeting a challenge (as by increased effort or improved performance)

stretch *verb.*
- straighten or extend to full length to reach something

Why Read a Book About Stretching and Growing (Up)?

Last year, while working with a leadership team on building capacity using the ideas in my book *Swimming in the Deep End,* I suddenly realized I had not emphasized a fundamental foundational idea. One cannot lead effectively without modeling what it means to be a professional, and it's also important to model what it means to be changing and growing oneself as well as stretching one's learning edges and developing. Leaders must walk the talk.

But there was pushback. "Why do I have to model this?" they cried. "Shouldn't everyone already be there already?" I heard more resisting and frustrated comments from workshop participants. "My colleagues signed a contract. Our work shouldn't be about them. They should already be professional." This idea that educators are already 'fully cooked' continued. I read similar thoughts on a Facebook group post: "Working in a middle school and the adults are acting like middle schoolers. (I swear puberty in April is contagious)." Educators' exasperated words kept coming: "I don't understand why some adults don't know how to adult" and "Lots of teachers I have been around this year mix their assumptions with emotions, and it plays a huge part in their being seen as unprofessional."

I don't disagree, and yet... While there is a bottom line in terms of a level of professionalism that should be expected in our schools, growing up is never—and should never—be finished. We should always aspire to be better selves. The concept of being done with growing up assumes that those with whom we work are complete. Humans are never done developing. Adulthood can be a time of tremendous growth. And our schools can and should be places where everyone—not just students—learns, matures, and develops. We should not be in the child-development business but instead in the human-development business.

As educators, we speak about the importance of lifelong learning and continued growth and development. No matter how old we are or what we do, we recognize the need to continue to grow, and that should be expected of ourselves and our colleagues. We are all on a learning edge in one way or another. To stretch and engage with those edges should be a consistent practice—where we learn and unlearn.

A culture of adult learning helps everyone achieve. Continued learning is mentioned in job descriptions in many fields. There's good reason that professional development is embedded in many school, district, and province teaching standards in North America and elsewhere. And developing ourselves beyond teaching our grade levels or our subjects isn't something we often encounter in coursework. The concept of professionalism prominently features in teaching standards worldwide, but we don't focus much on defining professionalism. The idea of studying professionalism remains on the periphery—it's an expectation without support.

The frustration of those who post on social media about adulting and professionalism show us that workplaces must get better at supporting employees in terms of development—of growing (up) at work—beyond the foundational level. We need to move from bottom-line accountability toward personal responsibility. Helping teachers with asking themselves: How am I developing myself to have a greater impact on my school, in my community, and in my field? and Am I becoming more self-monitoring, self-managing, and self-modifying? and Am I growing (up)?

We have good reason to be become more developed human beings who are able to think with more complexity and manage ourselves during uncertainty and with compassion and greater awareness. We are living in a world where civil discourse across political lines is so challenging that many have checked out. We are living in societies shaped by colonialism with systemic and institutional racism, and we deal with inequities of tremendous proportions in and outside of our school buildings. We are in need of minds and hearts in conversation in order to move us forward.

While I'm writing this, the Covid-19 vaccine has just begun shipping, many of us are still in lockdown, and we will be wearing masks for a good while into the future. Many students in our schools are learning at a distance, missing classmates and the experiences they imagined they would have. Many are experiencing deep trauma in their communities and homes. Students need us to provide as much support as we can. Adults have been stretching themselves and need to continue to stretch in ways nobody expected and yet are essential.

My work on stretching at one's learning edges emerged within this context. Yet I believe this will be a book that is useful and important beyond this moment. We will always need to be in conversation with ourselves and strengthen our ability to do so. This book assists those in schools to think about child development and adult development. As Felipe Fernandez-Armesto said in *Humankind: A Brief History*, "If we want to go on believing we are human and justify the special status we accord ourselves—if, indeed, we want to stay human through the changes we face—we had better not discard the myth (of our special status), but start trying to live up to it."

California Professional Standards for Educational Leaders

Element 5A: Reflective Practice
Leaders act upon a personal code of ethics that requires continuous reflection and learning.

Example Indicators:
5A-1 Examine personal assumptions, values, and beliefs to address students' various academic, linguistic, cultural, social-emotional, physical, and economic assets and needs and promote equitable practices and access appropriate resources.

5A-2 Reflect on areas for improvement and take responsibility for change and growth.

5A-3 Engage in professional learning to be up-to-date with education research, literature, best practices and trends to strengthen their ability to lead.

5A-4 Continuously improve cultural proficiency skills and competency in curriculum, instruction, and assessment for all learners.

5A-5 Sustain personal motivation, commitment, energy, and health by balancing professional and personal responsibilities.

UK Teaching Standards

- Fulfill wider professional responsibilities.
- Make a positive contribution to the wider life and ethos of the school.
- Develop effective professional relationships with colleagues, knowing how and when to draw on advice and specialist support.
- Deploy support staff effectively.
- Take responsibility for improving teaching through appropriate professional development, responding to advice and feedback from colleagues.
- Communicate effectively with parents with regard to pupils' achievements and well-being.

Who Should Read This Book?

This book is for readers who want to level up and stretch themselves. It is for anyone who is on a journey of continuous self-improvement.

This book is for readers who want to consider how they can be even more inclusive in their thinking, their communications, and their actions. It's for those who want to engage in the conversations about equity, diversity, and belonging, and for those who want to develop skills, dispositions, and mindsets to do the important inclusion work in their schools and organizations.

Michael Fullan, in his book *Nuance: Why Some Leaders Succeed and Others Fail* writes about those who have a "curiosity about what is possible, openness to other people, sensitivity to context, and loyalty to a better future." He writes for leaders who "are courageously and relentlessly committed to changing the system for the betterment of humanity." This book is for the reader who is relentlessly committed to changing systems for the betterment of humanity through the work of developing themselves.

In terms of roles, this is a book for the following kinds of people:

- Teachers, administrators, and coaches;
- Team members;
- Anyone leading a team (grade levels, departments, schools, district) who wants support and language to use as they build group capacity.

Regardless of role, this book will help you expand your repertoire and skill set around five key facets of adult development, drilling down to behaviors in daily interactions. Readers will find a language about facets that anyone can stretch and will develop an understanding about what to expect from colleagues in interactions. The end goal is for readers to develop ways to articulate what behaviors look like and sound like as they amplify what development can be.

We need to support ourselves and our colleagues where we are and as we stretch forward. We can do so through conversations. Actions and interactions can remind us and encourage us as we ask "Why?" and help us support our students by not only talking our talk but also by better walking our walk. Former California State Senator John Vasconcellos once said, "We must become both hospice workers to support the peaceful dying and letting go of our traditional culture of fear and cynicism, and midwives to gently usher in our emerging culture of trust and mutual regard and with it a more hopeful future." When we go into education, none of us signs up for being a hospice worker or a midwife, but there are times that we are both—helping people let go and helping people birth new ways of being. This book helps us "to gently usher in our emerging culture" and assist us with accompanying one another on the journey of development and growth.

How Is This Book Organized?

This book is straightforward. After exploring the framework's foundation and how the five facets came to be, readers will delve into each facet's chapter. There is no order to the facets, nor are they distinct from each other in real life. There is much overlap, and as you begin to develop and find your learning edges in each one, you might notice that growth in one area generates growth in others. The facet chapters have common features, such as continuums, self-assessments, and reflection questions.

INTRODUCTION: WHAT DOES IT MEAN TO GROW (UP) AND STRETCH YOUR LEARNING EDGES?

What do I mean by "growing up" and stretching one's self at one's learning edges? This section introduces Robert Kegan's adult developmental theory and asks how adults continue to develop throughout their lives. The chapter explains the idea of stretching on a learning edge and leveling up (growing (up)) within the five facets in the book.

CHAPTER 1: FACET #1—KNOW YOUR IDENTITY

How can we know ourselves deeply as an individual, a colleague, and a teammate? What should we know about ourselves as we work with others? By acknowledging and knowing our history, upbringing, strengths, biases, limitations, motivations, and values, we can become better and more aware colleagues and teammates.

CHAPTER 2: FACET #2—SUSPEND CERTAINTY

How do we stretch beyond ourselves and build our intellectual humility and perspective taking? Being able to suspend certainty that we are "right" enables us to see outside ourselves and reflect on and critique our own decisions and value systems. These qualities are essential to work effectively as a team member and a more inclusive and equity-minded colleague. This facet looks at being open minded to others' ideas, realizing we don't see a whole picture, and maintaining a balance between advocating and inquiring.

CHAPTER 3: FACET #3—TAKE RESPONSIBILITY

How can we take responsibility for our own work product, our language, our actions, and our development? This chapter considers how to face challenges directly and humanely with an intent to work out solutions, and apologize when we have been incorrect or hurtful. This facet includes taking responsibility for our own personal and professional development and that of the profession as a whole.

CHAPTER 4: FACET #4—ENGAGE IN RECIPROCITY

This chapter reminds us of our responsibility to work together respectfully while recognizing that we cannot accomplish major feats in siloes. It asks what skills it takes to see the big picture and to work with collaborative expertise, and what skills are needed in order to live with a sense of equality and mutual respect in our team and supervisory relationships. What do we need to do show our belief in the worth and dignity of those with whom we work and the communities we serve?

CHAPTER 5: FACET #5—BUILD RESILIENCY

The work we do is challenging and demands resiliency. Chapter 6 focuses on several questions: What emotional and psychological hygiene must we practice to be healthy for ourselves and for others? How do we sustain commitment, energy, and health for ourselves and our work? How do we build the bandwidth to feel more comfortable with life's ambiguities and disappointments?

CHAPTER 6: WHAT NEXT?

Here the book deepens the understanding of how the five facets are interrelated and how we can continue to develop throughout our adult lives. Where do we go from here to continue the journey? We can't take a detour, we have to move forward and continue inner conversations with ourselves for greater outward impact. Stretching on one's edges and growing (up) is a never-ending journey. The discomfort will continue!

What are the Key Pieces of This Book? How Do I Use Them in My Development?

There are common pieces in each chapter:

- Guiding questions to frame the reading;
- A continuum to assess your learning edges. It outlines foundational characteristics (not an exhaustive set) and identifies likely behaviors at different stages of development. The idea isn't to journey through the continuum as quickly as you can. You can live a productive and happy life never having placed left a specific spot on the continuum; the question is to ask yourself if your work asks something different from you that is found at a different stage on the continuum.
- Self-assessments to help find your learning edges and determine your degree of awareness regarding any specific facet;
- A self-talk graphic that illustrates what you might say about yourself or others at each stage of development. These questions may give you a sense of where you are in your growth within any facet and raise questions to ask at another time on your journey;
- Exercises to support your development in a facet. Use exercises in each chapter for self-reflection, group reflection, or in a book study. They are not busy work. Each supports development as a professional and human being. You will build awareness, stamina for reflection, and the ability to move forward in your growth;
- Reflection questions to use for book studies or self-reflection.
- There are also quotes to inspire, text boxes of research for further study, and links for videos, books, and additional resources interspersed throughout each chapter.

Here are some ways to work with specific parts of the book:

THE CONTINUUM

Each continuum has foundational characteristics of the facet (not an exhaustive set) on the left. From left to right is a set of likely behaviors at different stages of development. The intent of the exercise is to self-reflect and consider how these skills make you effective at your job. As you review the continuum, make notes as to why you place yourself in a specific box at this time.

Remember:

- Characteristics of the facet are listed on the left.
- There is no order to the characteristics. All are important for your development at any given time.
- Developing yourself is messy and extends across a lifetime. Like life, your progress won't be a continual move from left to right.
- You might change boxes depending on situations and find that your development isn't linear. Moving in both directions along the continuum is common, and situational context matters.

THE SELF-TALK GRAPHIC

Another way to look at the characteristics of each facet is to experience what self-talk might look like. What might you say to yourself or to others at each stage of knowing your identity?

THE SELF-ASSESSMENT

Another way to interrogate your development is by self-assessing behaviors that align with related characteristics. What might you do or say if you were progressing through the stages? For each statement, you'll select the response that most represents where you feel you are. After you circle your responses:

Look. Look for patterns. Where are you most aware/least aware?

Reflect. Which statements surprise you and merit future thought and attention?

Consider. How might learning more about yourself in response to these statements support your development and assist you in your work?

EXERCISES FOR DEVELOPMENT

All exercises align with the facet and its dimensions. There is no specific sequence for these exercises.

Remember:

- These are intentionally called 'exercises' rather than 'activities.' The goal is to develop in each facet and that development takes a building of an emotional and cognitive muscle. Hence, exercise is the chosen word for defining these types of experiences.
- You can decide which exercises align with your specific focus for each facet. You can do some of the exercises or you can do them all. Self-determination rules.

- There is no expectation that the exercises be done perfectly; there is no perfect score.
- There is no time limit on how long any exercise should take.

WAYS YOU CAN READ THIS BOOK

This video is a quick visual explanation of Jennifer going through the ways you might consider working with this text so you get the most out of the experience.

https://bit.ly/3ctgcGE

GUIDING QUESTIONS AND REFLECTION QUESTIONS

Guiding questions begin every chapter and could be used as an activator to surface prior knowledge and connect to the chapter's content. They could be journal prompts or discussion starters. The reflection questions at the end can be used as prompts to integrate learning and scaffold the key takeaways.

CONCLUSION

Our schools can be and should be inclusive and promote belonging of all who teach and work and study in them. All schools stretch at their learning edges to acknowledge inequities due to institutional practices and policies. This work asks us to commit to stretching ourselves and examining how we need to change and develop individually and collectively. And there is so much more to do. I keep asking myself who am I now, who do I want to be, what affect do I have on my students and my colleagues now, and what affect do I want to have on the schools where I work and the field I serve? With this commitment at the top of my mind and a conviction in my spirit, my moments of feeling wobbly, uncomfortable, and messy in my development continue and I can manage them.

The world challenges all of us socially, politically, and environmentally. The need for self-awareness in all our interactions and especially in our schools is paramount. There are many more facets to being a more developed human being than are addressed in this text. I have much more to learn and to develop in myself. I often write a book so I can learn about something I don't know enough about, and I create a book that is a size too big for me.

Rabbi Abraham Joshua Heschel said, "What we need more than anything else is not textbooks but text people." I am living out loud my hope that we all become more developed, and I write with the aspiration we can continue to become more whole human beings. And so I hope this book contributes to the conversation.

Onward.

INTRODUCTION
What Does It Mean to Grow (Up) and Stretch at Your Learning Edges?

Education isn't something you can finish.
—Isaac Asimov

When I think of growing (up) or stretching at a learning edge, I see the act of stretching one's self—moving from being subjected to what's happening to engaging more objectively—to relate to the world in a different and bigger way. It is why I write "growing (up)" with parentheses, because it can be seen as a vertical development. One is getting taller with one's development (being able to see not only from the dance floor but upstairs from the balcony) but also developing in terms of breadth. It is to see more—more broadly—in the viewfinder with bigger lenses. So while I say "growing (up)," I could also say "seeing a bigger picture." This subject to object shift in how one sees the world is a critical attribute in many theories of adult development. I am not just driven by or swept by (or subject to) what is going on around me but I can look at my world outside me (more objectively) and then choose how I want to respond with more discernment and less reaction. Moving from one way of orienting to or making meaning of the world to another broader, more complex way of making meaning enables you to step up, and to step back – to better analyze and to better reflect on your best next step, to operate from a wider perspective.

Stretching at your edges requires inner and outer work. Find your "learning edges" where you are working to see more and to hold more. Act out of your proximal development zone—working on skills you are close to mastering (Vygotsky, 1978, p. 86). Rather than having your growth being driven through external guidance, you can find your own learning edges and bring about self-growth. You can master your own potential. By taking this stance of choosing to be on a learning edge, you will be able to:

- better see challenges as outside yourself;
- not be subject to or swept up by challenges;
- be less reactive;
- be more collaborative;
- be more thoughtful;
- live in the world with more equanimity.

These are skills that benefit not only you as an individual in your own world, but you as a member of a school or district or board. You can identify how your views shape your actions and can suspend your certainty about what is right in order to become a more compassionate, whole, and able human being who takes responsibility for how you contribute to your team. You can realize your own potential, and that benefit extends beyond yourself. You can increase your sense of efficacy and your ability to improve working relationships with colleagues. You can face adversities with aplomb.

Jenni Donohoo (2017) and Steven (2019) have written extensively about the positive effect that teacher efficacy has on student learning. Anthony Bryk and Barbara Schneider (2002) show how relational trust among colleagues makes a difference in student achievement. A strong sense of respect, personal regard, and more are needed to create a psychologically safe environment that promotes learning for everyone. Research finds collective efficacy is essential for the work of schools (Hattie, 2018).

A group's growth, and a school's effectiveness, relies on individuals stretching at their edges and becoming more socially aware, psychologically mature, and cognitively capable. In this way our personal efficacy can contribute developing that psychologically safe environment we hear about. Our personal resourcefulness can contribute to the collective efficacy of our groups which can make a huge different in our school community.

While some workplace actions are easily defined as right or wrong (financial malfeasance, sexual harassment, emotional abuse), individual development is more than what an authority figures tells you to do. When you begin a job or a black-and-white task such as learning to drive, there's nothing wrong with focusing on the rules. Rules keep us on our side of the road. They keep us physically safe and moving in one direction. Closely following the letter of the law, however, cannot be the goal for everything. We must develop beyond that. To be professionals and adults in our schools, we must be able to collaborate with others in challenging moments when guidelines are less clear, to see a bigger picture, manage ourselves through uncertainty, recognize how our upbringing affects our choices, and know how to find our voice in respectful way when we are disappointed and unsure. We need to challenge and confront systemic racism and work toward eliminating inequities in our school systems. We need to push ourselves to do better. We need to be bigger selves.

Individual growth is too complex to be mandated or delivered to a group in a PD session or a set of sessions. Each of us needs to grow (up) by questioning ourselves and stretching at our own edges. We need to grow psychologically and learn about ourselves and what we think, and we need to further develop our own judgment and discernment. Structures, systems, and professional learning opportunities and learning communities can ask us to interrogate ourselves and our work and enhance our abilities and practices to some degree. Yet each person on a team needs to engage at a different place, confront their edges, and inquire inside. "Where am I at the limits of my knowing? Where am I stuck? What can I do to stretch myself? How might I grow?" By doing so, one individual's development can elevate the group's work to a higher level.

We all have heard the adage: you can't teach an old dog new tricks. We know that doesn't have to be true! Our capacity to grow and change in adulthood is remarkable. Our brains are adaptable in ways scientists have discovered in only the last several decades. Each time we learn a new task, we change our brain. Adult brains are able to grow new neural networks. This idea of neuroplasticity means our brains are wired to continue to change if we challenge ourselves with new learning. A well-known study of London taxi drivers demonstrated that a driver's hippocampus—the part of the brain associated with learning, memory, and emotions—changes the longer a person is on the job because navigating the convoluted streets is particularly challenging. We are capable of adapting and advancing throughout our adult lives in ways never previously thought. We can progress and we can support each other on this development journey.

Foundational Beliefs of Growing (Up)

- We need a different *orientation* as the world and our work in education become more complex.
- We can realize our human *potential*.
- We can *grow psychologically* after we are done growing physically.
- We continue to *develop* even as we get older.
- We can broaden our sense of *meaning making* and how we interpret situations and experiences.
- We are able to build our own ability to *transform qualitatively*.

Let's consider our growth in schools and districts through a developmental lens. Robert Kegan's adult developmental theory offers a frame to guide our thinking. Kegan is professor emeritus at Harvard University and author of books including *In Over Our Heads: The Mental Demands of Modern Life,* and with Lisa Laskow Lahey, *How the Way We Talk Can Change the Way We Work: Seven Languages for Transformation* and *An Everyone Culture: Becoming a Deliberately Developmental Organization*. He has written about adult development for decades. His theory extends human development from child development into the range of adult development. You might have read about Abraham Maslow's hierarchy of needs or Lawrence Kohlberg's stages of moral development in children. Kegan also describes the ability for individuals to have qualitative transformations in their mindsets and abilities. In his theory, Kegan posits that adults orient to and make meaning of the world in four ways of thinking as they develop: self-sovereign; socialized; self-authoring; and self-transformational. Others have theories as well—Wilbur, Torbert and Cook-Greuter among others—and all share the belief and assertion that development in adults is possible, and development moves along a progression even when accounting for moments of fall back or spiraling down and back up. While others use different words to describe progress and some divide up stages differently, Kegan's theory's structure will be a frame for this text and will become our shared language. These are Kegan's four meaning-making orientations:

- **Self-Sovereign Mind.** The self-sovereign mind operates in black and white; there is no gray. Its emphasis is on the I and what I want. It is difficult to understand that others might see the world differently. Comfort is in the known. Not knowing something is very disconcerting. The self-sovereign mind finds it challenging to understand abstract concepts such as loyalty, faith, tradition. Not cheating is driven by fearing consequences rather than valuing honesty.

- **Socialized Mind.** A socialized mind relies on external scripts provided by family, friends, mentors, higher education, the school handbook, etc. It's difficult to personally articulate what is right from what the organization says is right. A socialized mind is swayed by others' views. Understanding doing something right is tied to external feedback. One's internal compass is not fully formed.
- **Self-Authoring Mind.** A self-authoring mind has identified personal beliefs and values and can question the expectations and values from the external world. It can articulate what is important, set limits, and solve problems based on internal beliefs. The self-authoring mind might resist the idea that personal beliefs could be wrong. This mind is more self-governing and doesn't like it when choices or personal theories are challenged.
- **Self-Transforming Mind.** A self-transforming mind is comfortable with tension and ambiguity and has moved beyond the idea that the truth is found only internally, which creates an openness to new ideas and perspectives even if these ideas are actively challenged. A self-transforming mind is interdependent; it takes the best of other ideas and integrates them with its own. This mind sees itself as part of a bigger world of gray and competing ideas, tensions, and paradoxes.

Schools and other organizations in human-centered professions offer rich opportunities for the work of developing and supporting others in their growth, and also for developing and maturing the human beings who work within them. Three orientations are most common for adults in human-centered professions (such as education, medicine, and social work): socialized, self-authoring, and self-transforming. This book will focus on stretching yourself on the leading learning edges connected to these three of Kegan's orientations.

I do want to mention that considering these ways of knowing, and progressing and moving from smaller to bigger ways of seeing the world, is not to suggest that one orientation is better or worse than another. Every way of knowing has positives and limitations. There are healthy parts at each stage and positive parts to different ways of making meaning of the world. And there are moments when we start feeling the limits of how our current way of orienting to the world is working for us. The world sometimes feels more complex and harder to understand within our way of making meaning. We need to stretch. A learning edge calls.

Throughout development, hopefully one includes and integrates the best aspects of the previous orientation in a healthy way. The lenses through which we see the world get bigger and bigger, and we are able to hold more complexity. Adulthood can be a time of tremendous growth and learning, and that can be uncomfortable for a time. Like molting—shedding skins—we need to let go of one way of seeing things so we can grow bigger. And workplaces can be supportive containers for that growth.

VIDEOS

To learn more about adult developmental theory, view these videos:

Transformative learning through the lens of constructive developmental theory, featuring Dr. Ellie Drago-Severson, Teachers College, Columbia University.

https://bit.ly/38QrnXB

Collection of videos featuring Dr. Robert Kegan, Harvard University.

https://bit.ly/3lnvX4L

Adult development map featuring Dr. Jennifer Garvey-Berger, author of *Changing on the Job*.

https://bit.ly/3rn6EBh

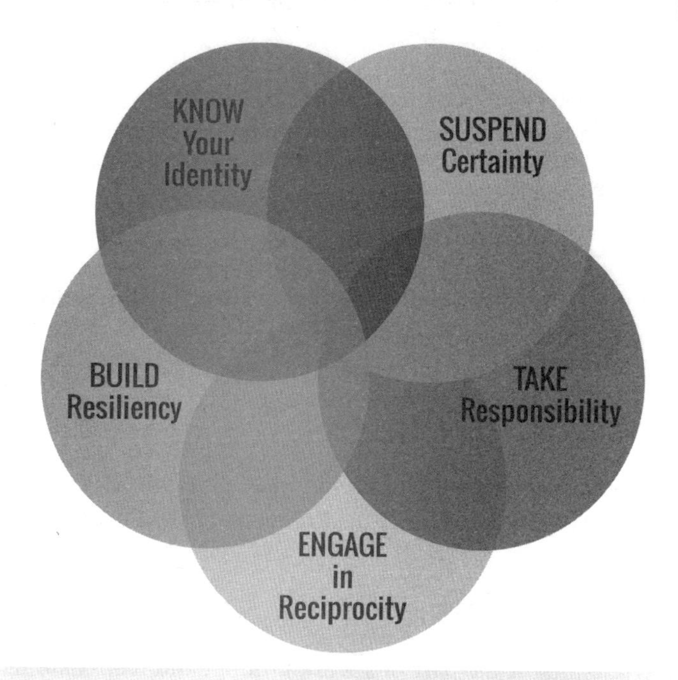

The Five Facets of Growing (Up) at Work

The five facets of growing (up) at work mentioned in this book developed out of the socialized, self-authoring, and self-transforming orientations and with the foundational beliefs outlined here (see sidebar).

> **Foundational Beliefs of Growing (Up)**
>
> - We need a different *orientation* as the world and our work in education become more complex.
> - We can realize our human *potential*.
> - We can *grow psychologically* after we are done growing physically.
> - We continue to *develop* even as we get older.
> - We can broaden our sense of *meaning making* and how we interpret situations and experiences.
> - We are able to build our own ability to *transform qualitatively*.

As I work with groups domestically and internationally, I often find that team members from the San Francisco to Toronto, Istanbul to Cape Town, and Prague to Porto Alegre, all faced similar challenges. Difficulties emerged in team members becoming defensive during discussions; in recognizing the challenges of teaming with others over time; and in supervising a colleague struggling to manage adult-to-adult interactions in the workplace.

It's essential to become more aware of privilege and power and more inclusive in our thinking, communicating, and our how we act in classrooms and when interacting with students, families, and colleagues. We need grow and develop ourselves to become anti-racist and anti-oppressive in our systems, policies, and practices. We cannot bypass the hard inner and outer conversations we need to have with ourselves and with each other. Kegan (with Laskow Lahey) mentions in *Immunity to Change: How to Overcome It and Unlock the Potential in Yourself and Your Organization* (Cambridge, MA: HBP, 2009, p. 54) that we all have bumped up against "the limits of our current ways of knowing," and we know in our bones that we need to stretch ourselves to move beyond. We can be in fellowship around this work, however, and accompany each other as we journey forward.

I began to identify facets that I believe we need to develop if we want to be more successful in our schools, our professional interactions, and in our career trajectory. These mindsets, capacities, and skills coalesced into five facets—buckets within which to categorize an individual's developmental journey. These areas are where we can continually develop and stretch our learning edges. They are broad enough to allow for continual personal growth in each one, and by working on each facet over time, you will see they are interconnected and interact with each other while helping you become a better teammate and colleague.

In this book, the facets are separated for discussion purposes, but consider the Venn diagram with blurred edges and overlapping interdependence.

These are the five facets.

FACET #1—KNOW YOUR IDENTITY

- I know myself, my history, my biases, my values, my limitations, and my motivations. I know how my upbringing and my experiences impact my work with colleagues and students.

FACET #2—SUSPEND CERTAINTY

- I have the ability to remain open to multiple possibilities and multiple points of view. I am prepared to be wrong, and I own my limitations and fallibility.

FACET #3—TAKE RESPONSIBILITY

- I take ownership for my part of a work product and responsibility for how I interact with others and for my personal and professional development.

FACET #4—ENGAGE IN RECIPROCITY

- I recognize it is part of my job to understand my interdependence with others in the organization, and I work to collaborate well as I grow my skill set to do so. I demonstrate respect for all stakeholders within the organization and live out loud my belief in the dignity and worth of all.

FACET #5—BUILD RESILIENCY

- I work on my own emotional and psychological hygiene to be healthy for myself and for others. I build up my bandwidth to become more comfortable with the ambiguity of my work. I manage my disappointment and sustain my commitment to the work ahead.

With each facet we can ask ourselves:

- How do I live this facet out loud?
- In which situations am I more successful in embodying the best parts of this facet?
- Under what conditions does this facet feel shaken?
- What do I notice that could get in the way of doing this facet well?
- How might I address the challenges I face in this facet?
- What can I do to help me progress, stretch, and grow (up) in my development?

Your school, team, or grade level can join you on this journey. Everyone working in an organization is interdependent. We cannot accomplish our mission without one another's support and assistance. In this book, our energy is directed not on our content (our grade level or our subject), but on our process and development.

Schools can be centers to engage people of all ages. They enable us to contribute to society through teaching and also can support our development so we flourish as well. Schools can fulfill their mission by developing those who work for them—supporting administrators and teachers in becoming better professionals in our roles and for our students and better human beings. Developing ourselves in order to support students and also one another means we can work more productively, more meaningfully, more healthfully, and more purposefully. Wherever you are at this point in the text, you have opened yourself to your journey of self-discovery, and your goal of being a better self at school has already begun.

Define Your Learning Edges: Reflection Questions

- What main idea resonates with me from this introductory chapter?
- Which ideas do I feel most comfortable with at this moment? Which ideas currently stretch my thinking?
- Which of the foundational beliefs do I share?
- What will I try to take forward into my work from this chapter?
- At this moment, what idea from this chapter do I see as most worth my time?

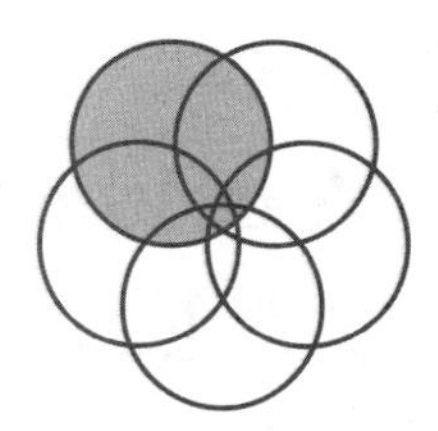

CHAPTER ONE
Facet #1 - Know Your Identity

It takes courage to grow up and become who you really are.
—e.e. cummings, American poet

CHAPTER TAKEAWAYS

As you read, consider these reflective questions and make notes of your takeaways.

- Which ideas in this chapter resonate the most with me?
- What seems most worthy of my time?
- Which concepts from this chapter have been the most meaningful and stand out for me to consider further?

Guiding Questions

- What role might my identities play when I work in collaborative groups?
- How do I self-identify? Which parts of my identity are more important now than they were in the past and which are less important?
- Where are my blind spots in terms of how I see the world? What don't I notice? Where are my limitations?
- Which parts of my identity would I like to learn more about?
- Which parts of my identity have the strongest effect on how I see myself in my personal life and in my professional life?
- What do I know about how I see the world differently than others? How do I work effectively with those differences?

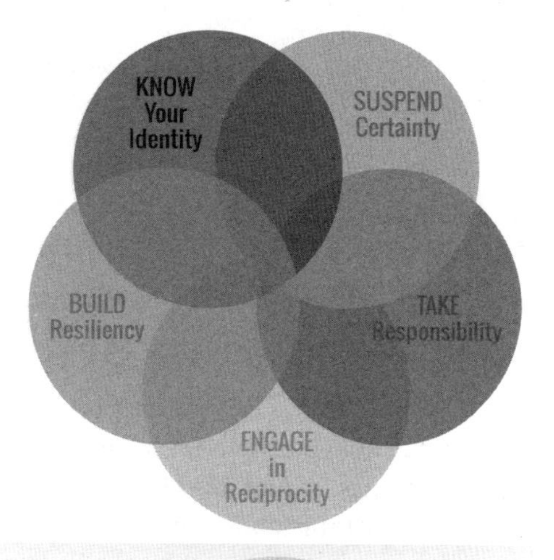

Definition: Knowing Identity

The skill of recognizing the condition or character as to who a person is or what a thing is; the qualities, beliefs, etc., that distinguish or identify a person or thing.

Facet #1: Know Your Identity Definition		
What It Is	**Why It Matters**	**What It Looks/Sounds Like**
Knowledge of your history and upbringing, as well as how your background informs your identity, beliefs, and values, and thus, your work. Recognition that your strengths, motivations, work styles, and learning edges help you discern the best next steps to develop yourself so you are able to collaborate more effectively with others who might not share those traits.	Increases self-awareness and personal insight. Increases flexibility in your choices of what to say and do, when and how to communicate, and how to behave in more productive ways for the good of your organization.	Being able to articulate your connection with various parts of your identity (gender, race, ethnicity, faith, etc.) and recognize how those parts impact your choices and actions. Examination of beliefs and actions and how your choices can adversely affect others. Ability to articulate your values, work styles, and preferences and recognize how those affect your work and leadership.

Know Your Identity: Key Concepts

"The unexamined life is not worth living." So said Socrates as he extolled the importance of self-examination. Understanding who we are as an individual is vital to working productively within teams because our identity shapes our behaviors, our choices, and our actions. Our upbringing and values affect how we communicate—what we say and how and when we say it.

Knowing about parts of your identity and how you are different from others on your team opens your eyes to decisions your group makes that may adversely affect others, such as these examples:

- Deciding to meet outside the workday when a team member might need to pick up a child;
- Speaking up directly during a challenging discussion making others who learned indirect communication based on their cultural upbringing really uncomfortable.
- Asking someone to commit to something on a weekend without regard to religious practice and need for personal and family time.
- Supporting a Secret Santa event at the holidays that has been done for many years without recognizing that some members of the team don't celebrate Christmas.

It's important that we recognize how our own identities *interact with* and can *bump up against* others' upbringings, values, and beliefs. Someone who grew up with less might have a different attitude about spending group money or view a certain choice as more extravagant than a person used to unencumbered income. Someone might have experienced receiving praise in front of a group as inauthentic and awkward to receive as their country of origin didn't overtly place a high value praise in that form. Someone else grew up in a family that used silence as a supportive experience to say, "I am here for you and no talking is needed," whereas another one remembers silence as code for demonstrating anger and frustration.

We have different stories and histories. We hold assumptions and have blind spots. We need to examine how our identity impacts our work with others. The essence of this chapter is ask you to stretch and continue the journey to knowing yourself, knowing your values, and examining how your identity (or identities) shape how you work.

You might begin to feel uncomfortable as you move into this chapter. Many of us strive to minimize differences with the goal to avoid stereotyping and to keep harmony within a group. We have been taught to treat each person as an individual and recognize the essential humanity in each one of us. The ideas in this chapter do not counter the belief that we are all human beings and should be treated with respect. This chapter is an exploration of ourselves and how our ideas and behaviors are culturally grounded. We cannot (and should not) apply our wish to feel comfortable onto others and thus avoid discussions which minimize our differences. That can leave to a negative impact and result in not seeing each person as the individual we wish to see. In the end, it can go against our intention to treat everyone with respect. We need to stretch at this learning edge in order to truly examine how a lack of knowledge about our identity and a lack of time spent learning about others is unintentionally affecting our work.

Your upbringing, personal history, strengths, and learning edges all consciously or unconsciously make you the colleague you are. At the heart of knowing your identity are several dimensions.

Know Your Identity: Dimensions

KNOWING YOURSELF TAKES WORK

Knowing yourself is an ongoing journey of discovery, and it doesn't happen without commitment. We know from experiences with those older than us that aging does not necessarily increase self-awareness. It takes conscious effort to understand yourself. It is true that you have preferences or inclinations such as, "I like chocolate more than vanilla," or "I am a night person." But knowing yourself, your biases, your limitations, and how your upbringing affects your work and impacts your work with others—well, that requires internal study.

For example, exploring how your family communicated with your schools might help you understand your expectations of parent-teacher interactions. Understanding how your family dealt with conflict may help you recognize patterns in how you talk to colleagues about difficult topics. Recognizing your strengths and weaknesses on a youth sports team might help you understand your approach as a team member. We bring our past into our present. Awareness of how history impacts current work is a worthwhile endeavor, because knowing and evolving is an ongoing, active project. Increased awareness might cause us discomfort, and that discomfort is important as we develop and grow.

NATURE AND NURTURE AFFECT HOW YOU ARE AND WHO YOU ARE

Research makes clear that genetics *and* family dynamics (nature *and* nurture) play a part in who we are (McLeod, 2017). Our genes and upbringing are right there in our fingerprints and in how we look at the world. Nature and nurture shape how our identity matters in our current settings.

Family dynamics influence how we think, what we value, how we characterize what makes a good life, and how we define a good relationship. What did your family say about your childhood friends? Did they have opinions about where you should go to school and what profession you should go into? Did they support your choice of becoming an educator? Our upbringing often impacts our behaviors and expectations. And our upbringing impacts how we *should* behave. Did your family always avoid conflict or did they engage? Did they expect you to finish tasks or obligations or did they understand if you stopped something midway? Did they expect you to do your homework straightaway after school or was it okay to stay up late to finish it? These mindsets ooze from our past into our present. When we recognize this, we can choose to continue thinking and behaving a certain way—*or not*. I worked with a colleague who was asked to be a "better self" and choose to lower his voice in a specific situation after he expressed his opinion in a high volume and it had caused a bit of fear from others. He commented, "What can I say? I'm from New York." His boisterous responses had been accepted as part of who he is. His family of origin spoke loudly. At forty years old and in a different region, he spoke at a volume that others did not welcome. Some viewed him as arrogant. He believed and perceived that the way he had always been was just fine in the present moment. There was a gap between his understanding of what was okay in one situation and how that didn't translate to his current situation. He needed to disrupt his thinking and communicate in a new way in order to be more effective. Through understanding how his past influenced his current actions, he could modify his behavior to fit his new context. Recognizing how parts of your identity might fit with your current environment and where you might face a challenge is part of exploring this facet.

BEING AWARE OF YOUR BLIND SPOTS IS A GOOD THING—REALLY

Self-exploration is easier for some than others. Looking at our blind spots is an uncomfortable undertaking. You may uncover or rediscover parts of yourself that you don't love to acknowledge. For example, you might not have thought about offering food to students during the holidays because you were never food insecure. Or you always assume families can attend parent-teacher conferences because your parents were able to take time off. Or you might expect a basic understanding of Judeo-Christian references since you grew up going to church or synagogue. Identifying, acknowledging and, dare I say, admitting you have blind spots, weaknesses, or limitations offers areas for learning and ways to grow. You aren't alone. We all have stretch points that can make us more understanding. Recognizing common humanity can help us understand that we aren't "bad." We are all stumbling forward. Each of us is human and has blind spots, and at times we slip up. Understanding that we all are "works in progress" can help us become more self-compassionate and more empathic toward teammates. This book isn't "calling you out" for being unawake or unconscious but instead is attempting to "call you in" to recognize how we can all work together with more understanding.

> *A worldview is a wave, but not the entire ocean.*
>
> —Barbara Brown Taylor, *Holy Envy: Finding God in the Faith of Others*

YOU AREN'T JUST ONE THING; YOU CONTAIN MULTITUDES

Whitman wrote in *Song of Myself*, "Section 51," "Do I contradict myself? / Very well then, I contradict myself. / (I am large, I contain multitudes.)" We each contain multitudes. Different aspects of ourselves come to the fore at different times of our lives and within different contexts. All aspects interact to make you the complex and interesting person you are. And understanding how multifaceted you are can offer insight into the multitudes that others contain. For example, my Midwestern upbringing sometimes manifests in my love for fried cheese sticks, but more often I follow the diet more common to my California home and eat tofu. I enjoy both. You may see yourself as open-minded until you have a discussion that points out a contradiction in your thinking. A colleague has commented that in her childhood home criticism was more common than praise and now after raising several children of her own and reading research about balancing challenge with support she sees the value of both positive and constructive feedback. She sees value in both. Be curious. Intrigued. You are human. You contain multitudes.

IDENTITY ISN'T FIXED, AND YOU *CAN* CHANGE

We are all in the process of forming our identity. A friend, reflecting on his work in education, said he is a *very* different colleague at age seventy than he was at twenty-two. He has lived in a variety of locations, had children and grandchildren, and has dealt with health challenges. He is now focused on working to combat educational and financial inequities in society. This was of interest to him decades back but now has become a front-and-center true focus. Age changes us, as do life events such as moving, divorce, deaths, relationships, teaching, leading, raising children, and external events in the world. You shouldn't feel stuck with one identity, attached to the same passions, fears, thoughts, feelings, and limitations. You can ask yourself what story in your life brought you to any given opinion and whether you want to continue thinking this way. You *can* change and adapt. Perhaps you were always in favor of homework and were pro-suspension as disciplinary action. Over time, you raised a family and saw things from other angles and changed your opinion.

What we value and what we believe can also surface during transitional or challenging moments (sick leave, a move) or through new learnings as new roles are added (mother, caretaker). Our awareness of what matters to us can change in an instant. Historical and political changes happen. Health scares bring bodies into focus. Becoming a spouse or a parent can shift how we view the world and our role in it.

Our identity, whether conscious or not, shared openly or not, shapes our actions and our choices at work. We might want to focus on different projects, emphasize certain initiatives, or take on new tasks. We might want to change roles or redesign our career trajectory. We might want to engage with different individuals. When we develop our self-definition changes. Along the self-study and development journey, we come to see circumstances differently, and from that awareness can change our behaviors. Your ways of doing things isn't fixed. You can adapt.

What Else to Consider?

A few additional thoughts about connections between our identity at home and at work to consider:

- **Self-Identity and Belonging.** Your personal identity encompasses the qualities, beliefs, personality, and looks and/or expressions that make you who you are. People are members of various groups and become part of a collective identity. You may belong to a church, work for a school district, be a part of a neighborhood. Significant tension often exists between your personal identity and a group's collective identity. You may feel that the school you work for isn't as in sync with your belief system as you would like. You might want them to move to a certain assessment structure, allow more opportunities for all students, or provide more social-emotional supports. You grapple with the disconnect. How might you feel more authentic and still fit in at school? How you navigate tensions is a big part of the balance of wanting to be seen as part of a collective and yet maintaining individual identity and perspective with integrity. Internal struggles are common, and at times result in leaving a school district due to being out of alignment with the group's ways of seeing the world.
- **Self-Identity and the Workplace Identity.** Your identity can and most likely will be shaped by your school. As you are inducted into your school system or become a part of a team, your ways of being and communicating shift to become more like the group. You begin to take on the mindset and communication style of your team and school, and you act in accordance with group norms. Embodying group identity and incorporating it into how you think and speak goes beyond wearing your school's logo. You begin to embody a belief system (all of us should teach this way, etc.) and a way of being that your school embodies. While individuals influence the school system, the school system can and will deeply influence you. This sounds like the complete opposite of the previous paragraph. Any individual discovering herself in contrast to her workplace and the work of the organization shaping her is a both/and experience—they happen simultaneously. All systems have practices and routines and policies and structures, and they influence your mindsets and expectations of how schooling can and should happen. Does your identity gel with your school system in ways that support your goals for students and their families, and are you pushed in good ways to stretch at your edges?
- **Self-Identity and Home Cultures.** Our understanding of our own cultural identity develops from birth and is shaped by the values and attitudes prevalent at home and in our surroundings. Because we all need to feel accepted and comfortable within certain groups, cultural identity essentially relates to our need to belong. Working outside your country of origin brings your family identity and home country into bold relief. Third-culture kids (TCKs) born to parents of one culture and raised in another culture understand that navigating between and among cultures and ways of being can be a challenge and a skill. There is value in seeing the similarities between you and your organization as well as acknowledging and celebrating the differences. Again, we all work to hold tensions when they arise and make choices as needed.

DIMENSIONS—KNOW YOUR IDENTITY

By "choosing oneself among possibilities," as French philosopher Jean-Paul Sartre said, we reveal who we are. Through every choice we make, we not only reveal who we are, but we reshape our identities. We are always in the process of *forming* our identity.

Knowing more about ourselves is essential, and it's also not enough when it comes to being a more developed colleague and professional. We need to know the parts of our identity and to understand how we see the world differently than others do. The next chapter will move us from an inward-looking mindset into a more outward facing skill set—the ability to suspend certainty and understand where we might not see the big picture.

Facet #1: Know Your Identity Characteristics & Continuum

Characteristics	Stage 1	Stage 2	Stage 3
Knows there are many parts to a person's identity (personal history, race, culture, gender, and more).	I have begun the journey of acknowledging and naming the parts of my identity. I can articulate how my race, gender, upbringing, culture, etc. affect my work.	I can explain how different parts of my identity have stayed central in my adult life. I am just starting to articulate how my personal history and upbringing are in sync (or not) with systems, structures, and actions in my workplace.	I can explain how different parts of my identity have stayed central in my adult life and which parts are not. I can articulate how my personal history and upbringing are in sync (or not) with systems, structures, and actions in my workplace.
Intercultural awareness and development is essential for the work around diversity, equity, inclusivity, and belonging in any organization.	Recognize that I have blind spots in terms of my intercultural development, seeing inequities in my actions, and the system in which I work.	I can articulate and am examining, sometimes inconsistently, my biases. I am starting to pay attention to more of my practices and actions and how they are inclusive or not.	I am consistently interrogating myself and intentionally developing my intercultural awareness. I pay attention to my actions and their connection to equity, inclusivity, and belonging for all.
Knows that core beliefs and core values connect to one's work, either unconsciously or consciously.	I have begun to articulate my values and beliefs, and I can identify how these align (or do not align) with my work choices and actions.	I can articulate how a misalignment between personal and organizational values and beliefs creates challenges. I struggle but compromise when needed and begin to consider making a workplace change when I cannot (if possible).	I am aware that individuals have different values, and I advocate for my own beliefs while respectfully identifying others' values. I have developed strategies to navigate differences between personal and organizational values and beliefs. I help build a system that includes and honors my teammates' identities.
Is aware of strengths and weaknesses in regard to ability to collaborate with others and knows own preferred work style.	I am aware of my work style preferences (Myers-Briggs, colors, strength finder assessments, etc.). I can identify triggers that prompt judgment and negative reaction to working collaboratively.	I can articulate how my work style (Myers-Briggs, colors, strength finder assessments, etc.) differs from others'. I can self-monitor when differences arise. I attend to communication styles and adjust my style to communicate more effectively with others. I work to proactively manage triggers to maximize group productivity.	I am aware of my learning edges in terms of collaboration, and I have a toolkit of language skills and protocols to make sure all voices are heard. I honor and appreciate differences in workstyles, and I have strategies to resolve not only my own tensions, but tension within the group.

Facet #1: Know Your Identity Self-Talk by Stages			
	Stage 1	**Stage 2**	**Stage 3**
What am I saying to myself?	"I can explain who I am and the various parts of my identity to someone else." "I am not always sure that knowing my teammates as individuals is really important to the work at hand." "I have taken assessments to understand my workstyle. Does it matter? Hmmm." "I prefer that discussions focus on team tasks." "I struggle with conversations about bias." "Discussion about equity and inclusion are quite uncomfortable. I think we should minimize that type of conversation and respect everyone."	"I am aware of the parts that make up who I am, and I know how those parts fit (or don't) with the team." "I abstractly understand that exploring my blind spots is a good thing but it takes a lot of energy." "I know that I am one piece in the big puzzle that is my work-place. I recognize that I need to be aware of how to more effectively work with others and be less judgmental. And it is hard work." "My eyes are open to exploring my blind spots and biases and it's getting a bit more comfortable being uncomfortable." "When I am frustrated with how my team works, I am aware that I need to acknowledge differences in communication styles. I am stretched at my learning edges to work across styles and communicate my concerns more effectively."	"I am very much aware how the parts of my identity come forward in how I work with others." Albeit uncomfortable at times, I acknowledge how my limitations and biases affect how I work." "I intentionally seek opportunities to learn about others and their background in order to work inclusively." "I am curious about and compassionate toward my colleagues. I recognize that we all have stretch points." "I always ask myself, 'How could I be wrong?' and am consistently reflecting as I actively work to learn how to develop myself." "I recognize that my way is not the only way, the right way, or the best way. I seek out and explore my learning edges."
What am I saying to others?	"I admit I am judgmental or dismissive when it comes to sharing different perspectives. If the majority agrees then let's just keep moving." "I am not deliberately exclusionary. I don't know what I don't know and so just go with the mainstream." "I can be judgmental when I see alternate ways of doing things or different workstyles. I struggle at times when I am asked to consider that there may not be a 'right' way to do something."	"I have strong opinions about what the team should do and how to do it. I am confident about sharing my ideas and suggestions with the group. I am still learning to advocate but also inquire." "I am aware that intent isn't impact and my actions can have adverse consequences. I am working on my blind spots with intention." "I am stretching to learn about others' upbringing and styles. It's not easy."	"I am discovering more about myself and others. I am aware that I have blind spots and limitations. I take my self-study seriously, and I explore how I was raised and how I see the world as a result. I am aware of how different the world can look from other perspectives." "We all see the world differently and my intercultural awareness is ever increasing, as it is essential to work with more inclusivity and belonging." "I am compassionate and curious about others' perspectives. I often ask my teammates, 'What do you see from where you sit? What am I missing?'"

Know Your Identity: Self-Assessment

Another way to look at knowing your identity is by self-assessing behaviors that align with its related characteristics. What might you do or say if you were progressing through the stages of developing awareness around knowing your identity? For each statement, select the response that most represents where you feel you are.

- I can articulate clearly the most important aspects of myself. I have an "introduction" ready.
  - ☐ I haven't thought about it.
  - ☐ I have given this some thought, and I'm getting better at this.
  - ☐ I have given this a lot of thought, and I am very good at this.
- I am aware of possible differences between me and those with whom I am communicating.
  - ☐ I haven't thought about it.
  - ☐ I have given this some thought, and I'm getting better at this.
  - ☐ I have given this a lot of thought, and I am very good at this.
- I can speak to which parts of my upbringing and history continue to affect my life.
  - ☐ I haven't thought about it.
  - ☐ I have given this some thought, and I'm getting better at this.
  - ☐ I have given this a lot of thought, and I am very good at this.
- I can speak to which parts of my upbringing and history I have consciously chosen to minimize and can explain why.
  - ☐ I haven't thought about it.
  - ☐ I have given this some thought, I'm getting better at this.
  - ☐ I have given this a lot of thought, and I am very good at this.
- I can articulate how my upbringing aligns with my current values.
  - ☐ I haven't thought about it.
  - ☐ I have given this some thought, and I'm getting better at this.
  - ☐ I have given this a lot of thought, and I am very good at this.
- I can articulate how my values align with how I work and/or how I lead.
  - ☐ I haven't thought about it.
  - ☐ I have given this some thought, and I'm getting better at this.
  - ☐ I have given this a lot of thought, and I am very good at this.
- I can describe ways that I seek to understand how others view the world.
  - ☐ I haven't thought about it.
  - ☐ I have given this some thought, and I'm getting better at this.
  - ☐ I have given this a lot of thought, and I am very good at this.
- I incorporate an understanding of my group's background/upbringing diversity in my communications and actions.
  - ☐ I haven't thought about it.
  - ☐ I have given this some thought, and I'm getting better at this.
  - ☐ I have given this a lot of thought, and I am very good at this.

- I can describe ways that I am developing intercultural awareness and how my communications and actions support or hinder the inclusion and belonging of all my team members.
  - ☐ I haven't thought about it.
  - ☐ I have given this some thought, and I'm getting better at this.
  - ☐ I have given this a lot of thought, and I am very good at this.
- I have taken personality and work-style preference assessments, reviewed the results, and can describe connections between my "type" and my behaviors.
  - ☐ I haven't done this.
  - ☐ I have given this some thought, and I'm getting better at this.
  - ☐ I have done many of these, and I am very good at this.
- I have taken assessments, reviewed the results, and can articulate when I am challenged by other people's styles.
  - ☐ I haven't done this.
  - ☐ I have given this some though, and I'm getting better at this.
  - ☐ I have done a lot of this, and I am very good at this.
- I am aware of my pet peeves and triggers and have ways to manage myself more productively when I collaborate with others.
  - ☐ I haven't thought about it.
  - ☐ I have given this some thought, and I'm getting better at this.
  - ☐ I have given this a lot of thought, and I am very good at this.

Now that you have selected your responses:

Look. Look for patterns. Where are you most aware/least aware?

Reflect. Which statements surprise you and merit future thought and attention?

Consider. How might learning more about yourself in response to these statements support your development and assist you in your work?

Know Your Identity: Exercises for Development

All of these exercises align with the parts of the continuum and the self-assessment in one way or another. There is no specific sequence for these exercises. All thinking and reflection is good.

Remember:

- These are intentionally called exercises, in contrast to activities. The goal is to develop in this facet. This type of growth doesn't always feel good or easy.
- You can decide which exercises align with your specific focus within the continuum for this facet. You can do some of the exercises—or you can do them all. Self-determination rules.
- There is no expectation that the exercises be done perfectly; there is no perfect score.
- There is no time limit on how long an exercise should take.

EXERCISE 1: Identity Circle

Purpose: To help you recognize your various parts. Everyone comes to work each day with every part of them. The identity circle is a visual to use to begin a conversation to get to know all the parts of yourself.

Guiding Tips:

- This exercise is not intended to be an invasion of privacy or for sharing uncomfortable things. To start, explore the parts of the circle silently and individually. Ultimately you choose what to information to share with the goal of bringing more of yourself into work and creating an inclusive space for others.
- You may not know what a specific identifier means. For example, you may question what "ancestry" means or the difference between "gender identity" and "sexual identity." Before starting the exercise, you may want to look up definitions and then ask yourself how you would respond.

Directions: Look at the whole circle and the individual segments. Answer these questions. Take time to write down your answers.

1. If someone were to ask you about yourself, which parts of your identity as defined by the identity wheel would be *most immediate* in your response?

   ____

   ____

   ____

2. If someone were to ask you about yourself, which parts of your identity as defined by the identity wheel would be *less immediate* in your response?

   ____

   ____

   ____

3. Which parts of the identity wheel were more important to you when you were younger? Which parts do you expect will be more important as you age?

   ____

   ____

   ____

4. Which parts do you typically not think about? Which do you think about often?

   ____

   ____

   ____

BLIND SPOT

In this video Jennifer describes a moment when she discovered something important about her identity that was a blind spot for her.

https://bit.ly/39kEyQU

Post-Exercise Reflection:

Now that you have considered how you see the parts in this graphic, ask yourself these questions.

- What surprised me as I thought about my identity? What has my attention? What did I learn from this?
- If I knew how others would respond to the questions, how might that help me in my collaborative work and support us all in becoming a more inclusive team?
- How can I learn about my colleagues in a respectful and sensitive way?

Extension:

Have a conversation with someone at work who feels comfortable answering the questions above and share your responses with them. Ask them about theirs. What answers surprised you? What did you learn from the experience?

EXERCISE 2: Know Your Core Values

Purpose: To understand your identity and how you define yourself. Your identity and what you believe affects what you do—and don't do—in the workplace, and are therefore important in how you teach and lead. This exercise asks you to consider which values are most important to you and how you live them in your work.

Guiding Tips:

- This is not an exhaustive list of core values. Add any values you'd like. Many lists of core values can be found on the internet.
- You might think of different answers for different contexts (personal situations rather than work; a prior workplace rather than current). That's okay. Focus on your current work situation and be aware of differences based on context.

Directions: Determine which values are most important to you. Look at the list and choose your top ten values. In a second round, review your list and narrow it to your top five values. Once you have your top five values, write about how you demonstrate these values in your actions at work.

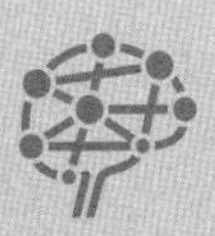

MORE ABOUT VALUES AND BELIEFS

The Virtues Project™ is a global grassroots initiative to inspire practicing virtues in everyday life. www.virtuesproject.com

YourMorals helps you learn about your morals, ethics, and/or values, while also contributing to scientific research. www.yourmorals.org

CORE VALUES

Authenticity	Citizenship	Fame	Knowledge	Pleasure	Service
Achievement	Community	Friendships	Leadership	Poise	Spirituality
Adventure	Competency	Fun	Learning	Popularity	Stability
Authority	Contribution	Happiness	Love	Recognition	Success
Autonomy	Creativity	Honesty	Loyalty	Religion	Status
Balance	Growth	Humor	Meaningful	Reputation	Trustworthiness
Beauty	Curiosity	Influence	Work	Respect	Wealth
Boldness	Determination	Inner Harmony	Openness	Responsibility	Wisdom
Compassion	Fairness	Justice	Optimism	Security	
Challenge	Faith	Kindness	Peace	Self-Respect	

____

____

____

____

____

____

Post-Exercise Reflection:

- How do you think your top five values affect your individual work and your work on teams?
- How might working with others who prioritize different values lead to policy challenges or conflicts? In schools, for example, there may be different views about what and how students should learn, or rules, or how social-emotional learning works alongside academic content.

EXERCISE 3: Professional Strengths and Weaknesses (from *The Multigenerational Workplace*)

Purpose: By expressing strengths and weaknesses and learning about those of your team members, you can become more productive. This exercise gives you an external focus to allow you and your teammates to safely explore and better respond without judgment. Use it to jump start a group discussion and possibly preempt moments of frustration.

Guiding Tips:

- This is not an exhaustive list of what you need to know about yourself or members of your team. Add your own pet peeves, triggers, requests, needs, or additional questions you find helpful.

Directions: Write down your answers to the questions. If an answer depends on a context or project, note those nuances. Circle the five questions you think are most important to share with your team in order for them to understand you better. Then circle the five questions for which you most want your teammates' responses.

1. Are you a "get things done right away" or a "give me a day or two to think about it" worker?

   ____

   ____

   ____

2. Which tasks do you enjoy doing with others? Which do you feel better doing on your own?

   ____

   ____

   ____

3. What are your strengths as a worker? What about as a coworker? What are your learning edges?

   ____

   ____

   ____

4. What motivates you at work?

   ____

   ____

   ____

5. What situations/challenges/work assignments do you most enjoy? Which ones challenge you most?

   ____

   ____

   ____

"Yes, you have obligations and responsibilities but, at the end of the day, if you don't know who you are, where your choices come from, and how to manifest a life of happiness, joy, and fulfillment, you may end up with regrets. The ability to pinpoint the specific things that derail your behavior helps you regain control of your mind and emotions, enabling you to respond consciously and productively."

—Tris Thorp, leadership coach

6. How do you handle interruptions or a change in plans? How might someone best work with you in those situations?

____

____

____

7. Do you consider yourself more of an introvert or an extrovert? How might that change the way you approach something and in which situations?

____

____

____

8. If you have taken personality/work style/learning style assessments, what did you learn that others might find useful for working with you? For example, are you an introvert or extrovert; big-picture oriented or detail focused; nonlinear or sequential; concrete or abstract; decisive or open-ended; logical or intuitive?

____

____

____

____

9. What is the best way to communicate with you? By text, email, in person, phone, other?

____

____

____

10. Do you tend to write in a brief or more detailed way? What direction do you need to complete an assignment—a bulleted list of to-do's with deadlines or just a gist?

____

____

____

11. How will others know if you are hurt or upset? How do you want to be treated if you are?

____

____

____

12. Do you prefer to know well in advance about a project or are you okay getting a task closer to a deadline?

____

____

____

13. Do colleagues describe you as having rose-colored glasses or as someone who sees the glass half empty? How do you think your outlook affects how you work with others?

14. How do you prefer to handle mistakes? Yours or others'?

15. What are your strengths in a group? What can others count on you for—keeping others on track, bringing in other perspectives, other things?

16. What types of acknowledgment do you prefer—public or private praise, tangible gifts, other?

17. In what situations do you ask for help? How do you feel about asking for help?

18. How would you like to receive feedback? In what form?

19. What are your pet peeves when collaborating with others on a team?

20. Do you consider yourself a risk taker? In what areas of your life do you like to be spontaneous? In what areas are you more cautious?

21. How much of your personal life do you like to share at work?

____

____

____

22. Do you socialize with work colleagues? Do you enjoy having lunch with colleagues?

____

____

____

Post-Exercise Reflection:

- What did you notice about your answers that surprised you?
- How might sharing some of your answers with your team members help you and them?
- How might you use this set of questions to get to know others on your team in a new way?

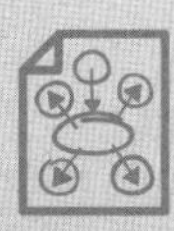

ADDITIONAL SELF-ASSESSMENTS

Compass Points Activity: An Exercise in Understanding Preferences in Group Work from National School Reform Faculty. https://bit.ly/3siihuw

The Myers-Briggs Foundation, Myers-Briggs Type Indicator. www.myersbriggs.org

CliftonStrengths, Strengths Finder. https://bit.ly/39bAa6I

True Colors. www.truecolorsintl.com

VIA Institute on Character, Survey of Character Strengths. www.viacharacter.org

Deloitte's Four Work Styles: Pioneers, Drivers, Integrators, and Guardians. https://bit.ly/3favJNb

Shirzad Chamine's Positive Intelligence, Saboteurs Assessment–How You Self Sabotage? https://bit.ly/3fbFCtS

The emotionally intelligent person knows that they will only ever be mentally healthy in a few areas and at certain moments, but is committed to fathoming their inadequacies and warning others of them in good time, with apology and charm.

—Alain de Botton, *The School of Life: An Emotional Education*

EXERCISE 4: What Threatens You?

Purpose: To learn what types of communications cause "verbal paper cuts." David Rock, neuropsychologist and author of *Your Brain at Work*, has written extensively about how the brain considers every interaction either threatening or safe. He identified five personal motivations—status, certainty, autonomy, relatedness, and fairness—and calls them the SCARF model. Learning to recognize your triggers—irritations during communications—can help you recognize when you are stung by specific conversations and consider wording in future communications.

PAPER CUTS

In this video Jennifer shares a story of how she connects personally to the SCARF model. Her SCARF Paper Cut Story.

https://bit.ly/3vZjbyh

Guiding Tips:

All human beings—no matter what age—seek recognition, certainty, control, belonging, and inclusion. *Everyone has all five of these motivations.* Some are more worried about these needs and may respond stronger when feeling threatened, but nobody is wrong or weird or overly sensitive for being driven by these motivations. When one of the five drivers is not present or is ignored or disrespected, you may feel diminished, discounted, or in the extreme, unsafe. Rock's five motivators are described in the chart below. Some are more important in general and others may come to the fore in specific contexts. Understanding your motivators is key to knowing yourself and what drives you.

Directions: Take the SCARF assessment found at https://neuroleadership.com/research/tools/nli-scarf-assessment/ to discover how the five motivations shake out for you.

Five Personal Motivations: The SCARF Model

STATUS	CERTAINTY	AUTONOMY	RELATEDNESS	FAIRNESS
The importance of one's self compared with others. Being of value, seen, acknowledged.	Ability to predict the near future.	Having some control over one's environment and actions.	Being "in" or "out" related to the social group; connection, belonging.	Having the same rules and procedures for everyone.

Post-Exercise Reflection:

Consider the results of the online assessment alongside these questions.

- What surprises you about the assessment results?
- What makes the most sense to you from the assessment?
- How aligned is your self-perception with the results?
- What new insights do you have about yourself, and how might they help you in your interactions?
- Does completing this assessment make you more conscious of others' needs, motivations, and concerns? What might you learn as a team by discussing this assessment?
- In what ways might the SCARF model help you be more mindful as you work with others?

EXERCISE 5: Looking at Your View of the World (Looking Through Your Prism)

Purpose: To bring to the fore how you might be a "fish in water" and not see cultural or national mindsets at work. If your team's or school's work emphasizes a different perspective than yours, you might experience anxiety or feel resistance. Geert Hofstede and colleagues conducted one of the most comprehensive studies about how worldviews influence how we live, do our work, and expect our workplaces to function. Hofstede writes about six dynamics (or lenses) one might face across cultures and dynamics that affect a work environment. For example, someone born in the United States and working in China might notice that their birth country and host country see the world differently when looking through Hofstede's six lenses.

Guiding Tips: Hofstede is one of many cultural expert voices. Some say he brings his Eurocentric point of view to his work. Be open to a discussion about these six differences as a starting point, and learn more by going beyond to other sources. You may find some questions confusing—as a fish might be confused if asked to describe water. That is okay. Try to be comfortable with any confusion. Remember, there is no right answer to these questions, nor is any response better or worse than another.

Directions: Think about the six types of cultural differences described below and then respond to the questions.

Hofstede's Six Dimensions

Power Distance—The degree of inequity among people.

- Is the culture you grew up in more hierarchical and unequal, or is it flatter with more equal status among members of society? How does the country you currently live in align or not align with your country of birth?

____

____

____

Individualism vs. Collectivism—The degree to which people prefer to act as individuals rather than as a member of a group.

- Does the culture you grew up in focus on your identity primarily as part of your family unit or was your community your primary connection?

____

____

____

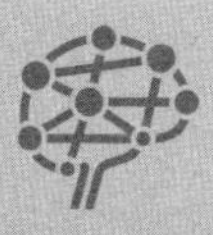

CROSS-CULTURAL UNDERSTANDING

Read about and then download the Hofstede Insights app. It offers the opportunity to use a comparison tool to compare country scores based on the six dimensions.
https://news.hofstede-insights.com/news/hiapp

Consult The Culture Mastery, LLC for more cross-cultural information.
theculturemastery.com

Masculine vs. Feminine—The degree to which values like assertiveness and performance prevail over values like service and care for the weak.

- Does the culture you grew up in value an assertive culture where speaking up is welcomed, or did it value nonconfrontation and avoidance?

____

____

____

Uncertainty Avoidance—The degree to which people prefer structured over unstructured situations.

- Is the culture you grew up in okay with ambiguity and big decisions being out of your control, or is it more disciplined and prescriptive so little is left to chance?

____

____

____

Long-term vs. Short-term—Compromise, obligations, and modesty are emphasized over individual values, rights, and winning in any given situation.

- Does the culture you grew up in favor tradition and keeping things the same across generations, or does it favor change?

____

____

____

FRAME OF REFERENCE

In this video, Jennifer speaks about discussions she has had with those who live in other countries and how her US 'centric' frame of reference has been highlighted in those conversations.

https://bit.ly/2PW2GlK

Indulgence vs. Restraint—Freedom and personal happiness emphasized over controlled and more rigid behavior.

- Does the culture you grew up in accept pleasure and celebration, or does it advocate control and restraint? Is bringing personal opinion or stories of your personal life valued and accepted at work, or is expressing oneself vulnerably or more intimately saved for more personal and informal situations?

____

____

____

Post-Exercise Reflection:

- What surprises you? What thoughts do these six dimensions prompt? What insights did you gain?
- Have you considered these ways of moving through life, or are they new to you?
- How might your understanding or beliefs about what is “acceptable” or “unacceptable” affect your work, your leadership, or your view of policy and procedures in the workplace?

> *The most dangerous worldview is the worldview of those who have not viewed the world.*
>
> —Alexander von Humboldt, German naturalist

EXERCISE 6: How Do You See the World? Interviewing a Colleague

Purpose: To understand more about a colleague's values and worldview. Use the conversation to explore a colleague's identity.

Guiding Tips: Approach this conversation with a mutual understanding that neither person's worldview is more correct than the other's. Neither of you is "ahead" or "behind." Conduct the interview with compassionate curiosity.

Directions: Ask your colleague to meet with you and answer these questions together. When you more clearly understand different points of view, you can collaborate more effectively in the future.

- Look at the identity circle graphic from Exercise 1. Which of the parts of your identity are most important to you or best describe you? What is most immediate? How do you think these parts affect your work in the classroom and your work in the wider school culture?

  ____

  ____

  ____

- When you look at the list of values in Exercise 2, which do you hold most sacred? How do you describe how those values connect with your work?

  ____

  ____

  ____

- When you look at the questions from Exercise 3, what do you feel is important to share with others about yourself?

  ____

  ____

  ____

Post-Exercise Reflection:

- What did you learn about your colleague that is helpful to know for future interactions?
- What did you learn about yourself from this interview process?

SOCIO-ECONOMIC WAKE UP CALL

In this video, Jennifer shares a story in which she learned yet again about how socio-economic differences impact one's view of the world. A socio-economic wake up call.

https://bit.ly/3slhK58

EXERCISE 7: The Kaleidoscope of Filters

Purpose: To understand more about how you see or don't see personal bias or understand cultural difference.

Guiding Tips: Consider these questions as part of your intra-personal reflections and for future inter-personal conversations around intercultural competence. These reflections are a part of an ongoing developmental journey. To contemplate in this way requires humility (and this is where this facet interconnects deeply the with other facets, especially a need to suspend certainty).

Directions: Write down your answers.

- **Societal Identity**—How do you connect or not connect with the country in which you live and with the region in which you work? You may describe connections in any way that you feel is appropriate.

  ____
  ____
  ____
  ____
  ____

- **Race/Ethnicity Identity**—How do you identify yourself in terms of race and ethnicity, and how do you see those identifications play out consciously and or unconsciously in your work?

  ____
  ____
  ____
  ____
  ____

- **Organizational Identity**—How do you connect or not connect with the organization/district/school where you currently work? Describe these similarities and difference in any way you feel is appropriate.

  ____
  ____
  ____
  ____
  ____

- **Department Identity**—How do you identify with your job description and your department? How do you connect with other departments in the organization?

  ____
  ____
  ____
  ____

- **Team Identity**—If you are on a specific departmental or cross-departmental team, how do you connect or not connect with that team and its goals and purpose as well as in the way you collaborate and communicate.

____

____

____

____

____

- **Individual (inter- and intra-personal)**—How do you see yourself as a work in progress and how does your intercultural competence development impact your identity?

____

____

____

____

____

Post-Exercise Reflection:

- What did you learn that might be helpful for your future interactions?
- How do different identities cause internal friction for you? How do different identities cause external friction amongst colleagues? How so?
- How might this exercise and exploration support your work and communications going forward?

It's not just about making our schools reflect our students' diversity. It's about representing identities that may join (or emerge from) our community. And it's about learning to see, respect, protect, and empower all of the identities we may encounter. #identitycenteredlearning.

—Daniel Wickner (@DanielWickner), Twitter, 12/11/20

EXERCISE 8: Sameness and Difference—Designing Wordles

Purpose: To understand more about how sameness and difference are both valuable in teamwork.

Guiding Tips: Consider these questions part of your self-conversation and future conversations around intercultural competence. Developing intercultural awareness is an ongoing journey. It requires vulnerability and humility, and this exercise highlights that knowing your identity interconnects deeply with suspending certainty and engaging in reciprocity (discussed more in future chapters). You can do this exercise solo, with a partner, or with a group. And you can do this through Wordle or Sli.do if participants are online.

Directions:

1. On a clean piece of paper, draw a box with four parts/squares.
2. Label the top left box "Upsides of Sameness."
3. Label the top right box "Upsides of Difference."
4. Label the bottom left box "Downsides of Sameness."
5. Label the bottom right box "Downsides of Difference."
6. Starting at the top and going left to right, add words that you feel align with the boxes. Examples:

Upsides of Sameness: Comfort, Ease	Upsides of Difference: Learning, New energy
Downsides of Sameness: Boredom, Fake	Downsides of Difference: Overwhelm, Anger

7. Then place an X in the box where you feel most comfortable at the moment.

   Ask yourself and your teammates:

   - What do you notice?
   - How might this exercise support your team to see the upsides to doing things in alignment and/or doing things autonomously?
   - How might this exercise support your team to see comfort and discomfort around equity, inclusion, and belonging conversations?

Post-Exercise Reflection:

- What did you learn about yourself that is helpful for your future interactions?
- How do these four concepts cause friction for you and your team? How do these different concepts assist you with increasing belonging amongst colleagues on your team? How so?
- How might this exercise and exploration support your work and communications going forward?

ADVICE FROM A CATERPILLAR

"The Caterpillar and Alice looked at each other for some time in silence: at last the Caterpillar took the hookah out of its mouth, and addressed her in a languid, sleepy voice.

'Who are *you*?' said the Caterpillar.

This was not an encouraging opening for a conversation. Alice replied, rather shyly,

'I–I hardly know, sir, just at present—at least I know who I was when I got up this morning, but I think I must have been changed several times since then.'"

—Lewis Carroll, *Alice in Wonderland*, Chapter V

If you want to identify me, ask me not where I live, or what I like to eat, or how I comb my hair, but ask me what I am living for, in detail, and ask me what I think is keeping me from living fully for the thing I want to live for.

—Thomas Merton, *What I Am Living For: Lessons from the Life and Writings of Thomas Merton*

AS YOU GROW UP . . .

"You recognize how your distinctive past colors your response to events and learn to compensate for the distortions that result. You accept that, because of how your childhood went, you have a predisposition to exaggerate in certain areas. You become suspicious of your own first impulses around particular topics. You realize—sometimes—not to go with your feelings.

You learn that part of what maturity involves is making peace with the stubbornly childlike bits of you that will always remain. You cease trying to be a grown up at every occasion. You accept that we all have our regressive moments – and when the inner two-year-old you rears its head, you greet them generously and give them the attention they need."—from the School of Life Collective, www.theschooloflife.com

FACES AROUND THE WORLD

An inspirational video of faces of humanity worldwide. YouTube video made/uploaded by jarray42, SupremeNomad

https://bit.ly/3mlwaFT

Chapter Reflection Questions: Know Your Identity

- What parts of my identity have I discovered?
- What stories in my life have brought me to my current identity?
- What forces have most shaped who I am?
- What aspects of my identity help me contribute the most to group work?
- What aspects do I need to be aware of when working on a team?
- In what ways might I contradict myself? (I contain multitudes.)
- What parts of my identity would I most like to work on? What parts do I most want to celebrate?

"He allowed himself to be swayed by his conviction that human beings are not born once and for all on the day their mothers give birth to them, but that life obliges them over and over again to give birth to themselves."—Gabriel García Márquez, *Love in the Time of Cholera*

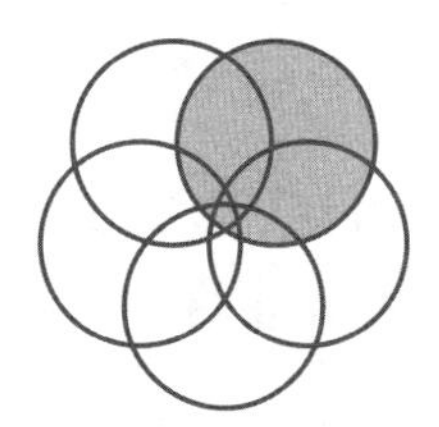

CHAPTER TWO
Facet #2 - Suspend Certainty

In the course of my life, I have often had to eat my words, and I must confess that I have always found it a wholesome diet.

—Winston Churchill, former prime minister of the United Kingdom

CHAPTER TAKEAWAYS

As you read, consider these reflective questions and make notes of your takeaways.

- Which ideas in this chapter resonate the most with me?
- What seems most worthy of my time?
- Which concepts from this chapter have been the most meaningful and stand out for me to consider further?

Guiding Questions

- In what areas of my life am I most curious?
- What are some benefits of being curious and inquisitive?
- What are some negatives of being curious and inquisitive?
- What surprises me most when others have a different perspective on something? What is my response (internally and externally) at those moments?
- How do I seek others' input so I have a fuller picture of any given situation?
- In what situations have I realized I didn't have the whole picture, which resulted in less optimal outcomes?
- How does intellectual humility show up in my life?

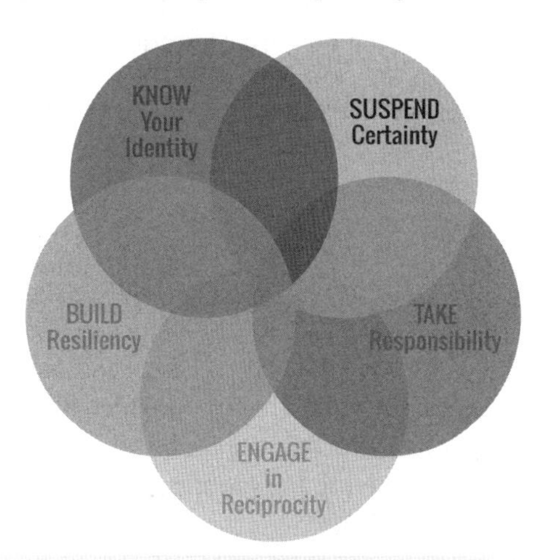

Definition: Suspending Certainty

The ability to set aside an opinion, decision, or perspective and hold it in an undecided state while awaiting further information.

Facet #2: Suspend Certainty Definition		
What It Is	**Why It Matters**	**What It Looks/Sounds Like**
Having an appropriate sense of self-regard; keeping things in perspective. Knowing you always don't know the bigger picture. Managing yourself respectfully in moments of uncertainty and ambiguity. Asking questions of others in order to understand their viewpoint and listening to those perspectives without immediate response or defensiveness.	Increases your understanding and awareness of limits in your thinking. Ideas, beliefs, and behaviors are culturally grounded and may be blind spots you need to learn more about. Seeing the bigger picture creates a more thoughtful group decision. Helps you become more curious and open-minded by seeing multiple perspectives.	Maintaining an open mind; listening without defensiveness to another point of view. Consistently asking, "What am I missing?" Not discounting or explaining away too quickly. Admitting mistakes and being able to apologize if defensiveness gets the better of you.

Rabbi Alfred Bettleheim once said: Prejudice saves us a painful trouble, the trouble of thinking.

—Justice Ruth Bader Ginsberg, *My Own Words*

Suspend Certainty: Key Concepts

Having ever increasing knowledge of one's self and one's identity is essential to adult development. And to continue on the journey of growing (up) and becoming an integrated individual and effective professional requires the sturdy ability to suspend certainty. To remain open to multiple possibilities and multiple points of view. To not rush to judgment. Suspending certainty requires acknowledging that you could be wrong. You begin to recognize that your judgments, beliefs, ideas, and behaviors are grounded in your world view.

For example, looking at what and how you teach through a different lens, you might notice some things. Perhaps you reinforce a Western point of view by including only works by European or white authors or by teaching mostly through direct instruction that doesn't allow all types of learners to successfully access the curriculum. By acknowledging that your way (or the way you were taught) isn't always the right way (or the only way) helps you attune to a larger understanding of the world.

Suspending certainty also means being able to consider more ideas with more flexibility and considering long- and short-term implications of your actions and decisions. It can be difficult to see the big picture, possible challenges, or stumbling blocks for others that you might need to consider before taking next steps. For example, you may want to do a certain lesson, and you need to ask yourself how might it play out in terms of the class period's time restrictions (short term do-ability), how it fits in with the whole unit (alignment with long-term objectives), or how it fits in with required goals and outcomes (student graduation outcomes overall).

Between stimulus and response there is a space. In that space is our power to choose our response. In our response lies our growth and our freedom.

– often attributed to Viktor E. Frankl, Austrian Holocaust survivor, neurologist, psychiatrist, and author

When you are open to other perspectives and also embrace them, plus possibly modify your response, new ideas can influence your work for the better. Openness is part of what makes you a more developed individual and a more effective team member. Several key concepts shape the suspending certainty facet.

Suspend Certainty: Dimensions

ACCEPT NEW PERSPECTIVES BY EMPTYING YOUR CUP

EMPTY YOUR CUP

In this link, Jennifer shares the Zen story about 'emptying your cup' via video.

https://bit.ly/2Pbwj2F

Getting your ideas on the table and bringing your knowledge to a group can be valuable in the workplace. Sharing your expertise and knowledge supports organizational productivity and effectiveness. And there is great value in hearing others' ideas and learning from their experiences. Being open minded and balancing your voice and ear requires that you "empty your cup."

There's a Zen story about a master teacher and a scholarly student. The student visits his teacher, who serves him tea in the student's tea cup, pouring so much tea that it spills out of the cup. The student protests, and the elder responds, "You come and ask for teaching, but your cup is already full; I can't put anything in." Being like the student in the story is detrimental as an individual and a team member. Until you empty your cup and suspend your certainty that you already have all or enough of the answers, you cannot learn and grow. Suspending certainty means you advocate and inquire. You talk *and* listen. You actively seek out new perspectives from those who are younger than you, in different roles from you, with different ethnicities and races than yours. You can ask, What might the students think of this? Parents who speak English as an additional language? Colleagues who work in secretarial and custodial positions? How might I suspend my certainty that my point of view is accurate? By asking these questions, you leave yourself open to the new. You empty your cup.

HOLD YOUR IDEAS—LIGHTLY

Suspending certainty doesn't mean that you must entirely let go of your knowledge or your perspective. You have earned your degree or your administrative credential and your point of view is valid and your knowledge is hard won. Nor does suspending certainty and being intellectual humble require you to be okay with intolerance or expressions or acts of violence, or to racism, homophobia, or any other unacceptable action which go against our collective social contract with those in our workplace and through their unacceptable actions deeply detract from creating a space of inclusion and belonging for all.

Suspending certainty does require though that you hold your opinion *lightly* for a moment, even when you have a strong opinion. You need to develop your ability to move past reaction and move to response. We need to grow our mental muscles to mentally rotate opinions and perspectives to view them from more than one angle; to prod and push against them to determine whether they are solid and have merit. Suspending certainty requires of us the ability to ask others to examine an idea you hold dear and when they push against it you don't become defensive. Suspending certainty allows you see more than you otherwise might. Maybe your instruction doesn't meet the needs of *all* learners. Maybe the schedule you designed for one student isn't as supportive as it *could* be. Maybe the email you're going to send is needed, and also you'll review it once again for the language you choose.

Some of us are accustomed to others pushing and poking our assertions and having our information scrutinized (scientists, doctors on rounds, a team of attorneys arguing a case). In these instances, we are asked to verbalize and explain our ideas, and they are examined for the betterment of the outcome. Ideas are external to us and our being. In other words, the information we offer is separate from our identity. Many people, though, have enmeshed their identity with their ideas. ("The student cheated on *my* test. My colleagues are out to get *me*.") We in education believe deeply in our work and hold onto our beliefs strongly. This leads to fusing our ideas with our identities, and it gets us in trouble as a field. It is hard to separate *who* we are from how our *information* is received. We often become defensive when we feel that our ideas being questioned means who we are and what we know is being questioned. As educators, it is truly challenging to leave the expert/teacher-of-record role behind in order to become more of a learner and listener. It is hard to suspend our certainty, overcome our defensiveness, and separate our identity from our ideas. And it is also essential that we do.

For example, I am a woman, so if someone suggests a different way to do a task, I might immediately think, "Would you have said that to a man?" Defensiveness is often a default because of a triggered memory of when someone said something to manipulate you rather than saying it with good intentions. Or if someone suggests that one of your beliefs is grounded in white privilege, you might immediately discount the comment or explain it away as you don't consider yourself to be biased. Defensiveness is a protective curtain that provides cover to those who understandably feel diminishing condescension. Suspending certainty doesn't require you to forget your past. It does mean you try to remain as open as you can and start by presuming the other person has positive intentions. Presuming positive intentions is to believe the other person is well-intended and trying to do the right thing. Anthony S. Bryk and Barbara Schneider's relational trust work and Jenni Donohoo's work on collective efficacy speak to the idea that when we demonstrate belief in our colleagues' good intentions, the group works more productively.

Stretching your mind and having your ideas questioned isn't easy. Yet being overly defensive isn't productive. Strive for a middle ground, neither clinging to one way of doing things nor letting go too easily of your point of view. Most importantly, separate your ideas from your identity and your ego from your intellectual development. Not easy, but worth the stretch.

LOOK THROUGH MICROSCOPES *AND* WIDE-ANGLE LENSES

One way to view your thinking is to see ideas from different angles. Thinking flexibly with micro and macro lenses changes your field of vision. Suspending certainty that you are seeing an idea the "correct way" and taking time to consider another point of view helps you see what you might have missed. Some chastise a focus on one way of thinking—describing it as "in the weeds," or "dotting i's and crossing t's," or "pie in the sky" or "only the big picture." Tones might be hurtful, yet this underlying caution is about viewing information from multiple angles. Your ability to probe an idea from multiple angles is a powerful skill in collaborative decision making. If you strive to spend time thinking through ideas using multiple lenses, you, too, can see new things.

TURN ON YOUR WINDSHIELD WIPERS

Like bugs coating a windshield, filters (beliefs, values, upbringing, opinions, ways of thinking) can blur your vision. Filters don't allow clear understanding in order to move forward. Did you know humans see only one percent of the light in the electromagnetic spectrum? Using that as a metaphor, imagine what you aren't seeing in the world. The same is true for interactions. Our filters, opinions, and biases obscure our picture of the world. Ask yourself, "What am I not seeing?" "Where am I unconscious?" "What film and blurriness do I need to wipe away so I can see better?"

Suspending certainty presumes that you use your windshield wipers. You strive to put yourself in situations and learning experiences that stretch you to set aside filters in order to see more. For example, attend professional learning opportunities about implicit bias, seek perspectives outside your field, attend webinars about topics that make you uncomfortable, watch films foreign to your country of origin, or read books by authors from other parts of your country or born in another country. Recognize that you are a fish swimming in water you cannot see.

> *One doesn't have to operate with great malice to do great harm. The absence of empathy and understanding is sufficient.*
>
> —Charles M. Blow, American journalist and *New York Times* columnist

SAY "BOTH/AND"

Children on a playground seesaw take turns going up and down. You, too, balance many aspects of your life: work and home, personal and professional, clarity and flexibility, alignment and autonomy. Sometimes you may long for the comfort and certainty of one way of doing things. You'd rather tilt toward that side and stay there. A seesaw doesn't work unless people are on both sides.

Suspending certainty and seeing not just one side of things but the "both/and" of your life is critical. People seldom face "either/or" decisions since we actually live in a "both/and" world. We need to hold two ideas without being able to reconcile them entirely. For example, how each country manages a global pandemic, maintains their economy, *and* keeps individuals healthy differs. Crises, such as the COVID-19 pandemic, requires precautions to stay healthy, such as masking and social distancing. Some businesses may not be conducive to those restrictions. However, solutions aren't an either/or proposition. It's not the economy *or* people's health. There are ways to accommodate both. Some want to "cross all the t's and dot all the i's," and others want to improvise solutions in the moment.

Don't let your seesaw get stuck in one position. Strive to suspend your certainty that your way is the right way.

EXCHANGE CERTAINTY FOR CURIOSITY

In recent years, I have often found myself startled, surprised, and dismayed by a comment that I strongly disagree with. My initial default stance was to immediately judge, disagree, and discount. I am growing to stretch myself from certainty and judgment to pausing and shifting to the question: "What can I learn here?" This is me working to suspend my certainty and shift to curiosity. Something that was invisible to me is now made visible.

Taking the time to recognize the possibility that something you might have been unaware of (an assumption or a belief or a bias) has surfaced will always benefit you in the end. Question your assumptions and assertions of how things should go or "how we do things around here." In meetings, ask, "Please say more," or "Can you elaborate?" or say, "I was missing that information." Doing that can go a long way to signal your desire to understand another's point of view. Curiosity fosters inquisitiveness and promotes divergent thinking.

Suspending certainty does *not* mean your assumptions are incorrect. Suspending certainty does *not* mean that you agree fully with another person's point of view. It means you are interested and curious about that point of view. Stephen Covey said we must seek to understand before being understood. Seeking more information or greater understanding does not necessarily mean you agree. In many situations, understanding another person's point of view helps you gain a more nuanced view of a problem, creates empathy for a different perspective, and possibly moves the conversation toward a compromise or a more civil "agree to disagree" stance.

DIMENSIONS—SUSPEND CERTAINTY

Accept New Perspectives by Emptying Your Cup

Hold Your Ideas—Lightly

Look Through Microscopes and Wide-Angle Lenses

Turn on Your Windshield Wipers

Say "Both/And"

Exchange Certainty for Curiosity

Learn the Difference Between Assertiveness and Arrogance

LEARN THE DIFFERENCE BETWEEN ASSERTIVENESS AND ARROGANCE

In the end, after pausing and asking for clarification and seeing an issue from another perspective, you may ultimately decide that you still stand for the idea or information you originally put on the table. You are confident that what you have to say is appropriate and what you believe is the right decision. Speaking respectfully with assertiveness is fine. Speaking with arrogance and attitude is not. You may need to apologize if your tone is imperious or you sounded defensive when someone questioned your point of view. You may notice nonverbal cues that you offended the other person. Perhaps someone begins to cry, hunches over, or grows silent. Stand for what you believe, but do so tactfully with linguistic savvy and good nature. Consider using sentences with periods at the end of them rather than exclamation points. There is a difference between two statements with different punctuation: "This is what I see" versus "This is what I see!"

Facet #2: Suspend Certainty Characteristics & Continuum

Characteristics	Stage 1	Stage 2	Stage 3
Is aware of differences in values, beliefs, and opinions.	I recognize my underlying beliefs and that they may be different from another person's.	I am able to reflect on and sometimes can critique my values, beliefs and opinions. I understand others might disagree with me but I really don't always understand how they could see things differently.	I acknowledge that my values, beliefs, and opinions factor into my decisions, and I try to make decisions with a deep consciousness of those values, beliefs, and opinions and how they may be different from another's.
Seeks others' perspectives and remains open to hearing divergent points of view, questions assumptions, and strives for and orients to perspectives beyond self.	I understand but may not always be able to demonstrate the need for me to act in ways that takes the organization's needs into consideration in addition to my own.	I acknowledge that flexible thinking is a key aspect of emotional intelligence. I can articulate that I might be missing other perspectives as I share my point of view, and I am able to form questions for others about what I don't see. I don't do it easily or without prompting, but I can do it.	I actively seek out diverse views on issues and actively work to increase my understanding of others' histories and beliefs. I actively use and participate in protocols that make sure all voices and perspectives are heard.
Listens to others' points of view and feedback with a sense of resourcefulness (i.e., isn't defensive or angry in reaction).	I understand that organizations should offer every person feedback. I understand that workplaces have standards and expectations for work product and professional behavior. I am aware that I will be told when there is a gap between expectations and my performance. I notice that I often feel defensive and emotionally tense when receiving feedback.	I consistently self-evaluate whether I use best practices without others' involvement in that evaluation. I am at the initial stages of seeking feedback, and I am working on self-management so I am less defensive when receiving input.	I value others' input. I seek diverse points of view. I self-manage with aplomb. I remain resourceful and open when offered feedback. I recognize and can put aside any tendencies toward defensive reactions.

Suspend Certainty: Self-Talk by Stages

Another way to look at the characteristics of this facet is to experience what self-talk might look like at each stage. What might you say to yourself or to others?

Facet #2: Suspend Certainty Self-Talk by Stages			
	Stage 1	**Stage 2**	**Stage 3**
What am I saying to myself?	"I struggle to articulate my stance around specific issues. I feel uncomfortable owning my own stance. I seek out others' assurance that they share my stance." "I am surprised and even shocked at times when others disagree me." "I have spent limited amounts of time with those I know don't share my opinions or values." "I find if someone suggests there is another way to look at an experience that I sometimes have a knee-jerk reaction and explain it away." "When I don't think the majority of the group feels the way one individual does, I discount that person's opinion."	"I have an awareness that what I believe might not be what all others in my group believe." "I stand apart from the group at times in regard to what I believe and how I go about doing my work." "I notice that I am surprised at certain stances others take but I stop myself from immediately reacting most of the time." "I am okay voicing my divergent point of view." "I intentionally spend as much time inquiring about other's points of view as I do advocating for my point of view."	"I intentionally place myself in situations where expect that I won't see eye-to-eye with others." "I am curious and inquire about others' points of view as I know I have only one perspective." "I know I don't know everything, and like when a group can tinker around and come up with different results once we hear from everyone." "I am becoming ever more comfortable with discomfort, such as speaking out even when I think I may be the only one to hold a particular view." "When I am in situations where others have a different perspective, I'm growing comfortable listening to different points of view."
What am I saying to others?	I don't ask, "What do you think?" often as I share my point of view. I seldom have conversations in which I comfortably say, "That never occurred to me. Hmm..."	I am learning to ask, "What am I missing?" I am learning to say, "I appreciate that you shared that. That was tough to hear, but was important to share," and "I am surprised but intrigued. Say more."	I often and easily ask, "How do you see it? What's your point of view on this?" I often and easily say, "Thanks for stretching me/us to consider more so we get a bigger picture out on the table." I ask, "What might I do next to sharpen or broaden my view?" "Where do I have a distorted way of seeing or what might be keeping me from seeing more?"

Suspend Certainty: Self-Assessment

Another way to look at suspending certainty is by self-assessing behaviors that align with its related characteristics. What might you do or say if you were progressing through the stages of developing awareness around suspending certainty? For each statement, select the response that most represents where you feel you are.

- I am curious when others disagree with me or provide another point of view based on their own background, experiences, or ways of looking at a problem.
  - ☐ I haven't thought about it.
  - ☐ I have given this some thought, and I'm getting better at this.
  - ☐ I have given this a lot of thought, and I am very good at this.
- I often ask myself, "How might someone else look at this?"
  - ☐ I haven't thought about it.
  - ☐ I have given this some thought, and I'm getting better at this.
  - ☐ I have given this a lot of thought, and I am very good at this.
- I often ask my colleagues, "What am I not seeing?"
  - ☐ I haven't thought about it.
  - ☐ I have given this some thought, and I'm getting better at this.
  - ☐ I have given this a lot of thought, and I am very good at this.
- I try to learn about others' points of view before sharing my own (by asking questions, using protocols, or through conversations).
  - ☐ I haven't thought about it.
  - ☐ I have given this some thought, and I'm getting better at this.
  - ☐ I have given this a lot of thought, and I am very good at this.
- I have a structure in my life for reflection (journaling, meditation, a check-in buddy, etc.)
  - ☐ I haven't thought about it.
  - ☐ I have given this some thought, and I'm getting better at this.
  - ☐ I have given this a lot of thought, and I am very good at this.
- I am open to experiences that challenge my own ideas and beliefs.
  - ☐ I haven't thought about it.
  - ☐ I have given this some thought, and I'm getting better at this.
  - ☐ I have given this a lot of thought, and I am very good at this.
- I'm working on separating my ideas from my ego when my perspective is challenged.
  - ☐ I haven't thought about it.
  - ☐ I have given this some thought, and I'm getting better at this.
  - ☐ I have given this a lot of thought, and I am very good at this.
- I'm learning more about being willing to take action and change my point of view, even when I get entrenched in seeing things my way.
  - ☐ I haven't thought about it.
  - ☐ I have given this some thought, and I'm getting better at this.
  - ☐ I have given this a lot of thought, and I am very good at this.

- I am working on receiving and delivering effective feedback and managing my responses to it so I am more curious, less defensive, and able to speak comfortably without upset in these moments.
  - ☐ I haven't thought about it.
  - ☐ I have given this some thought, and I am getting better at this.
  - ☐ I have given this a lot of thought, and I am very good at this.
- I consider past painful moments to be learning opportunities.
  - ☐ I haven't thought about it.
  - ☐ I have given this some thought, and I'm getting better at this.
  - ☐ I have given this a lot of thought, and I am very good at this.
- I recognize that I am limited in my experiences with those who see things differently than I do.
  - ☐ I haven't thought about it.
  - ☐ I have given this some thought, and I'm getting better at this.
  - ☐ I have given this a lot of thought, and I am very good at this.
- I work hard to remain open-minded and listen when others express alternative views, and I ask clarifying questions.
  - ☐ I haven't thought about it.
  - ☐ I have given this some thought, and I'm getting better at this.
  - ☐ I have given this a lot of thought, and I am very good at this.

Now that you have selected your responses:

Look. Look for patterns. Where are you most aware/least aware?

Reflect. Which statements surprise you and merit future thought and attention?

Consider. How might learning more about yourself in response to these statements support your development and assist you in your work?

"A great mystery about humans is that many times we confront learning opportunities with fear rather than mystery and wonder. We seem to feel better when we know rather than when we learn. We defend our biases, beliefs, and storehouses of knowledge rather than invite the unknown, the creative, and the inspirational. Being certain and closed gives us comfort, whereas being doubtful and open gives us fear."—Arthur L. Costa, *Learning and Leading with Habits of Mind*

> *Teach thy tongue to say I do not know and thou shalt progress.*
>
> —Rabbi Moses ben Maimon, twelfth-century Jewish philosopher, commonly known as Maimonides

"The only reason we don't open our hearts and minds to other people is that they trigger confusion in us that we don't feel brave enough or sane enough to deal with. To the degree that we look clearly and compassionately at ourselves, we feel confident and fearless about looking into someone else's eyes." —Pema Chödrön, Tibetan Buddhist nun and teacher, author of *When Things Fall Apart: Heart Advice for Difficult Times*

Suspend Certainty: Exercises for Development

All of these exercises align with the parts of the continuum and the self-assessment in one way or another. There is no specific sequence for these exercises. All thinking and reflection is good.

Remember:

- These are intentionally called exercises, in contrast to activities. The goal is to develop in this facet. This type of growth doesn't always feel good or easy.
- You can decide which exercises align with your specific focus within the continuum for this facet. You can do some of the exercises—or you can do them all. Self-determination rules.
- There is no expectation that the exercises be done perfectly; there is no perfect score.
- There is no time limit on how long an exercise should take.

EXERCISE 1: Journaling—Celebrate Suspending Your Certainty

(adapted from an exercise from d.school at Stanford University)

Purpose: To reflect on your ability to question assumptions and celebrate when you do, one of the key characteristics of this facet.

Guiding Tips: These sentence starters are only guides. Follow the intent and the flow of the storytelling in this exercise rather than following the stems *exactly.*

Directions: Take 10 minutes to write your thoughts in response to these journal prompts.

Think of a belief you felt strongly about or an opinion you had that you modified in light of new information. You became more open-minded. Fill in these sentence stems to tell the story of how you suspended certainty. Think of one personal story and one professional story.

- Once upon a time . . .

  ____
  ____
  ____
  ____

- And every day . . .

  ____
  ____
  ____
  ____

- Because of that . . .

____
____
____
____

- Until finally . . .

____
____
____
____

- And ever since that day . . .

____
____
____
____

- And the lesson is . . .

____
____
____
____

Post-Exercise Reflection:

How does it feel to write down how you changed your point of view? How did you build your receptivity to new ways of looking at the world? How might you continue to do so?

EXERCISE 2: Go Wide!

Purpose: To ask more questions that cause you to step outside a specific stance to see a bigger picture, one that pushes your frame further out.

Guiding Tips: This exercise might be uncomfortable for people focused on immediate tasks who try to stay in their lane. It can be overwhelming to see through a wide-angle lens outside your own role and responsibility. This way of thinking might feel as though it is out of your purview and too broad. Notice the discomfort. Try to stretch yourself.

Directions: Think about a decision you are making for a group or a meeting agenda you have planned. Stretch yourself with any of these questions that feel relevant. These questions ask you to think outside your assertion or decision. Write down your responses.

- How might others feel about the decision or choice I have made?

____

____

____

- What assumptions am I making about what is needed or not needed at this moment and by making this choice?

____

____

____

- What am I perhaps not seeing in terms of possible challenges the team might experience because of my choice?

____

____

____

- What might someone older/younger, from another department, at another level, or someone outside my workplace say about my choice?

____

____

____

- How else could I do this? What other paths might I pursue?

____

____

____

- Are there any reasons to doubt my choice or decision?

____

____

____

Post-Exercise Reflection:

- Did viewing your choice or decision with wider-angle questions help you see it differently? How so?

EXERCISE 3: Grow Your Awareness of Polarity Management

Purpose: To explore the idea of both/and thinking. Polarity management when facing challenges can support your development and asks you to suspend your certainty that your "side" is the right side.

Guiding Tips: Carefully read the introduction to polarity management in the directions and consider the difference between a problem to be solved and a polarity to be managed.

Directions: Consider this quote from Robert J. Garmston and Bruce Wellman's book *The Adaptive School: A Sourcebook for Developing Collaborative Groups.* "Polarities are ongoing, chronic issues which are both unavoidable and unsolvable. Attempting to address them through customary problem solving only makes things worse. These situations are not problems to solve; they are polarities that require effective management. Leaders, departments, teams, and organizations become more effective as they learn to distinguish between the two and deal productively with both."

Polarities in the workplace could include:

- **Autonomy and alignment.** How much flexibility does an individual get in terms of their work versus how much is mandated as identical to what others do?
- **Team relationships and team tasks.** How much meeting time does the team spend on group connections and how much on actions and planning?
- **Clarity and flexibility.** How much detail is provided about any given task and how much freedom do individuals have to move forward with agency?
- **Continuity and change.** What must remain as it has always been and what is changing?
- **Authenticity and fitting in.** What do team members need to give up in terms of who they are in order to be a part of the collective? How safe it is to be oneself in the group?
- **Candor and diplomacy.** In what ways do team members feel open to speak directly to an issue and in what ways does semantic sensitivity come into the equation?
- **Solitude and community**. When does the group allow for silence and time for individual reflection and when are opportunities created for the collective to join together?

These polarities are not "either/or." We need a "both/and" way to look at them; not completely discounting one side or the other. Like breathing, we need both to inhale and to exhale. Now, think of a new policy you have at your workplace. Or a roll out of a new initiative. Using the short explanation above, ask yourself, "How might I see this change from one pole?" And then ask yourself, "How might others see this change differently? Might their needs be on a different pole?" As you suspend your certainty, can you see that you are both right?

POLARITY MANAGEMENT: BOTH/AND THINKING

In this video, Jennifer shares a story from her consulting practice where she coached an administrator around balancing polarities in her work.

https://bit.ly/2QLfXOI

Post-Exercise Reflection:

- Did you notice that you are more comfortable seeing things from one side or the other of the polarity?
- Might looking through the lens of polarity management help you be a bit more open in your thinking and more understanding of the bigger picture?

"I know the term 'non-dual thinking' is still new or strange to many people. It simply means our ability to read the moment, to read reality in a way that is not judgmental, a way that is not exclusionary of the part that we don't understand. And it takes practice to learn that. It's very interesting that the term 'non-dual' is taken for granted in three of the Eastern religions: Taoism, Hinduism, and Buddhism. This word would be very familiar to them because it's the best descriptor of high-level consciousness—when you don't split everything up according to what you like and what you don't like. You leave the moment open, you let it be what it is in itself, and you let it speak to you." —Richard Rohr, Franciscan priest and author of *The Naked Now: Learning to See as the Mystics See*

EXERCISE 4: Language Skills—Advocacy with a Hint of Inquiry

(adapted from *Schools That Learn*, by P. Senge, et al.)

Purpose: To be able to advocate *and* inquire. Advocacy alone is not always a supportive skill. Taking a both/and approach, you share your point of view *and* inquire about how others see things.

Guiding Tips: Try to stick to the structure of the exercise. Having each sentence in its given place helps the listener track your thinking. Review your language for adjectives and adverbs that project defensiveness—words including always, never, only.

Directions: Choose a decision or a stance you feel passionate about and that you believe is the right next step. Complete all of the following phrases to build a structured and cogent assertion of your point of view. Notice when the sentence stems switch from advocacy to inquiry. After you have completed the stems, then write down your thoughts about how others might look at this point of view. (Be other-focused.) Finally, end your advocacy script with an inquiry. Using sentence stems, you may become more capable of articulating a stance (advocacy) *and* suspending certainty to seek feedback from others (inquiry).

1. State your assumptions/beliefs. Here's what I think...

____

____

____

LOOKING BEYOND A WESTERN PERSPECTIVE

In this video, Jennifer recalls an interaction with a colleague who identifies as Cree and her perspective how suspending certainty could be a learning that is needed by those with a Western perspective more so than in Indigenous cultures .

https://bit.ly/3udcEOZ

	Step	Prompt
2.	Describe your reasoning.	These are some reasons I arrived at this conclusion...

____

____

____

3.	Give concrete examples.	For example, I think about... and I think about...

____

____

____

4.	Reveal your perspective.	I acknowledge this is my stance on this and...

____

____

____

5.	Anticipate other perspectives.	Others might think differently and say...

____

____

____

6.	Acknowledge areas of uncertainty.	I am not that clear on this piece of the puzzle...

____

____

____

7.	Invite others to question you.	What are your thoughts?

____

____

____

Post-Exercise Reflection:

- How did you feel as you used this scaffold to organize your points?
- When you have advocated in the past, did you use a structure? What from this exercise is new to you?
- What do you notice about your language choices as you both advocate and inquire? As you prepare this script, what do you discover about your point of view?

EXERCISE 5: The Body Doesn't Lie

Purpose: To address our *physical* defensiveness so we have fewer negative responses and develop curiosity in challenging situations.

Guiding Tips: This is not an exact checklist. Don't try to do all these strategies in order to seem curious. Choose specific strategies that might help when you need support in order to stay present and curious, suspend certainty, and be less reactive.

Directions: Think of a moment when you felt hurt by feedback and your body responded. Did you cross your arms, squint, briefly hold your breath? Our body doesn't lie. We communicate micro-messages even when we try to remain open-minded. While we may not have a verbal outburst, sigh, or roll our eyes, our body follows our mind's reaction to the message and exhibits a defensive posture. Take several minutes to journal about that moment. Try to write about the moment from the first person as if you were sharing it with a close friend.

Now, with that feeling or that memory of that feeling in your body, review the strategies below.

As you read through the strategies, identify two strategies that if you knew about them at the time would have helped you feel less reactive and defensive.

Before the conversation would it have helped to:

- Use the Wonder Woman pose studied by Amy Cuddy by putting your hands on your hips and thrusting your chest forward. See Amy talk about the pose here: https://bit.ly/3ea5xAf While in the pose, breathe. Take at least three big breaths. Breathe in through your nose and out through your mouth. Take as long as you can with the inhale and the exhale—try a count of four to six. Would you have been helped by doing this prior to the interaction?

  NOTE: The research on the benefit of the Wonder Woman stance has been disproven in terms of shifting a listener's perspective. The other person may or may not determine that you are a strong person. I believe that the pose facilitates breathing and makes you feel powerful enough to handle what comes next, which is the benefit. The oxygen you take in to your upper body in those three breaths is physiologically calming and straightens your spine. (https://bit.ly/2OPcHRK)

- Create a mental bubble to surround you, at least one arm's length in front, behind, and on either side of you so you felt protected from others' energy penetrating your bubble.

- Place both feet solidly on the ground. Connecting to the earth. Do not crossing your legs. Making sure your spine would be upright and your body projects dignity.

During the conversation might it have helped to:

- Focus your attention on *what* is being said rather than *how* it is being said. When you recalled physical reactions that indicate a trigger (nervousness in your stomach, tension in your jaw, etc.), would it have been helpful to have acknowledged your reaction and invited it to sit beside you until the conversation is over?

- Tell yourself in the moment inside your mind, "This is a hurtful moment" rather than "I am hurt." And "This is a moment of anger" rather than "I am angry." Would it have helped to say, "This is a moment of sadness" rather than "I am sad." Cognitive behavior therapists and others suggest that by externalizing a feeling and separating ourselves from the feeling we are less subsumed by it.

After the conversation within the next hour or day would it have helped to:

- Think about what caused your reaction and ask yourself:
    - What feeling was triggered in me?
    - Which of my values did I feel was most threatened by this feedback moving forward?
    - What points in this interaction may be more important than fear and anger?
    - Can I separate the what from the who and learn something new?
    - What do I want to let go of?
    - What can be different in my response to feedback?
    - If I can let go of the emotion and drama, what one lesson can I take away?

Post-Exercise Reflection:

As you identified two (or more) strategies which might have helped you feel less reactive and defensive and thought about the use of them in that specific incident ask yourself the following questions.

- Did I notice any specific physical changes? Which ones? Give yourself a pat on the back if you are figuring out what to learn and how to receive input.
- Did the strategies help? In what way? What will I do again in a future moment in order to suspend my certainty or emotions for a bit longer?

EXERCISE 6: Man in the Mirror

(adapted from "13 Ways We Justify, Rationalize, or Ignore Negative Feedback," Peter Bregman, *Harvard Business Review,* Feb. 14, 2019)

Purpose: To take a balcony view of common defensive tactics and be able to name those that apply to you.

Guiding Tips: If you feel that every response in this exercise applies to you, you aren't alone. All of these are common defensive responses. If you don't see any that apply to you, perhaps ask a significant other or close friend how or when you have responded less than admirably when you felt attacked or received surprising feedback.

Directions: Think about a moment in a recent meeting when you responded to a challenge with defensiveness rather than curiosity. Make a check next to the responses you had—either out loud, on the phone later that night, in the parking lot after the meeting, or in your mind as you replayed the moment. By externalizing and naming your responses, you can identify them as defensive tactics. If you notice yourself saying something similar or thinking in these ways, your ego is keeping you from important learning. Suspending your certainty and your ego by not using defensive tactics can change your relationships.

In response to my behavior, statement, or idea being challenged, I said or thought:

- "Yes, that's true I said or did that, but it's not my fault." (playing the victim)
- "Yes, that's true I said or did that, but it was a good thing." (pride)
- "Yes, that's true I said or did that, but it's really not such a big deal." (minimizing)
- "I didn't do that/say that!" (denying)
- "Yes, that's true I said or did that, but you know what, I don't need to put up with this. I don't need this job!" (avoiding)
- "Yes, that's true I said or did that, but the problem isn't what I did, it's the people around me." (blaming)
- "Yes, that's true I said or did that, but there are lots of times when I did not do anything like that." (countering)
- "That may be true that I did this, but you did this thing, too." (attacking)
- "You don't really know anything about where I did or said that." (negating)
- "Yes, that's true I said or did that, but you know that is not the real issue." (deflecting)
- "Yes, that's true I said or did that, but I've asked others and nobody agrees with you and your perspective." (invalidating)
- "Yes, that's true I said or did that, who knew that makes me such a jerk?" (joking)
- "Yes, that's true I said or did that. You are right. I was terrible. I guess I'm really an awful person." (exaggerating)

Post-Exercise Reflection:

- In which situations have I made or do I see myself making any of these comments?
- How might I respond the next time I notice myself using one of these responses?
- How might I use this list to remind myself to put my ego aside? (Remember, it is okay to believe in your position and also to believe there is something to learn in the moment.)
- How will I remind myself that my point might not have been said as well as it could have been, and that my perspective might not represent the whole picture?

EXERCISE 7: Shared Multiple Perspectives Protocol

(adapted from National School Reform Faculty, nsrfharmony.org/protocols/)

Purpose: The purpose of this protocol is to give each person in the group an opportunity to have their ideas, understandings, and perspective enhanced by hearing from others. With this protocol, the group can explore an article, a text, etc. that merits deeper discussion and through the protocol the group can clarify their thinking, and have their assumptions and beliefs questioned in order to gain a deeper understanding of the issue.

Guiding Tips: For this protocol to be most effective, follow it exactly. Initially, the presenter shares a quote with no explanation. The facilitator should prevent any interruptions or cross talk. Some may chafe under these parameters, but the exercise offers tremendous payback if the protocol is followed.

Directions: Take 5 to 8 minutes for each round.

Protocol:

1. (1 minute) The presenter chooses a quote, data, or visual from the chosen text and directs the group to the page and section within that text that they personally want to explore. The presenter shares location of the quote from the chosen material so all can follow along at the presenter reads the quote aloud. Group members do not interrupt or share their feelings.
2. (1 minute) Starting with the person who is next to the reader in a clockwise pattern, the next person in the group responds to the chosen piece of text and shares their opinion, comments or thoughts about the writing – how it relates to him, what it makes him think of, etc.. No one interrupts or piggybacks on the response.
3. (1 minute per person) Repeat Step 2 until all group members have shared their reaction to the material.
4. (3 minutes) After everyone in the group has shared, the presenter explains to the group why they chose the material. The presenter also shares how the others' contributions changed or affected their original viewpoint.

Post-Exercise Reflection:

- What challenges did we face while using this protocol?
- How does this protocol support me in learning to suspend certainty?

PERSPECTIVE: SEEING SOMETHING BEYOND THE VIEWFINDER

"I've seen a lot of nasty posts in regard to people making 'non-essential' trips... Do you ever think maybe that guy buying a gallon of paint knows he must keep busy because idle hands in the past have caused him to relapse and pick up that case of beer? So he's using this time to do home improvements, something that keeps his mind busy while feeling a sense of accomplishment, trying to avoid painful triggers while possibly alone? Or maybe that lady buying bags of soil and seeds, hasn't struggled with depression and suicide? How do you know that planting and watching something beautiful grow during this time of darkness, isn't essential to her and holding on to what little hope she might still have? We need to remember that it is impossible to know just by looking at a situation from 'our' small lens what someone is truly going through or where their mental health is at. Everyone handles chaos and healing through different means, and I know we are all on edge but please stop being so judgmental of others. #mentalhealthisnumberone" —Sue Presler, Educational Consultant and Coach, Facebook, 4/9/20

EXERCISE 8: Conversation Inspired by Ralph Waldo Emerson

Purpose: To practice suspending certainty and listening in a small group context.

Guiding Tips: This conversation starter is most beneficial when group members have prior knowledge about each other and know what suspending certainty means. It can be used when the group is open to witness one another's development around this facet.

Directions: At the start of a conversation or meeting, use the Ralph Waldo Emerson query that he often used to open discussion at his salons, "What has become clearer to you since we last met?" Notice your response to what the other person says but do not comment. Ask yourself: When am I startled by something? When I am in alignment with the speaker? When do I feel surprised? Understanding? Frustrated? Irritated? What am I learning about myself through this process?

Post-Exercise Reflection:

- What topics came up?
- How well did I listen?
- What surprised me? Startled me?
- How did I manage myself so I remained present?
- What did I learn about suspending certainty?
- What are my strategies for staying "awake" and in a space of compassionate curiosity rather than judgment?

EXERCISE 9: Quotation Journaling

Purpose: To see how you and others are connected through and challenged by suspending certainty by journaling and sharing thoughts in response to the quotes on the list.

Guiding Tips: There is no right or perfect quote on the list. Pick one that most immediately connects to you in the moment or most challenges you at this time.

Directions: Take 5 to 10 minutes to respond to one quote. Also consider your a-has (insights), your hmms (ponderings), and your ouches (awareness of weakness) as you read the list.

- "Sometimes people don't want to hear the truth because they don't want their illusions destroyed."—often attributed to Friedrich Nietzsche, German philosopher
- "Losing an illusion makes you wiser than finding a truth."—Ludwig Borne, German writer
- "Knowledge rests not upon truth alone, but upon error also."—Carl Jung, Swiss psychologist
- "I tore myself away from the safe comfort of certainties through my love for truth, and truth rewarded me."—Simone de Beauvoir, French author

- "Sometimes I think I understand everything, and then I gain consciousness." —Ashleigh Brilliant, British author and cartoonist
- "When I am contradicted it arouses my attention, not my wrath. I move toward the man who contradicts me: he is instructing me. The cause of truth ought to be common to us both."—Michel de Montaigne, French philosopher and statesman
- "[T]he test of a first-rate intelligence is the ability to hold two opposed ideas in the mind at the same time, and still retain the ability to function." —F. Scott Fitzgerald, American author
- "If you aren't confused, you're not paying attention."—Tom Peters, American writer on business management practices
- "The other person is at least 10% right."—Anonymous
- "Let the filter work—ignore the blurt."—Michele Kuhns, American educator and consultant
- "What you can count on is that life will give you feedback. Now if you work at it, can you see it without ego?"—attributed to Chögyam Trungpa, Tibetan Buddhist meditation master
- "Sit down before a fact as a little child, be prepared to give up every preconceived notion, follow humbly wherever and to whatever abyss nature leads, or you shall learn nothing."—Thomas Henry Huxley, English biologist and anthropologist
- "Courage is what it takes to stand up and speak; courage is also what it takes to sit down and listen."—Unknown
- "Faced with a choice between changing one's mind and proving there is no need to do so, almost everyone gets busy with the proof."—John Kenneth Galbraith, Canadian American economist
- "The most difficult subjects can be explained to the most slow-witted man if he has not formed any idea of them already; but the simplest thing cannot be made clear to the most intelligent man if he is firmly persuaded that he knows already, without a shadow of doubt, what is laid before him."—Leo Tolstoy, Russian author
- "... truth exists only in the plural."—Gunter Grass, German author
- "Any upheaval in the universe is terrifying because it profoundly attacks one's sense of one's own reality."—James Baldwin, American author and essayist

____

____

____

____

____

____

____

Post-Exercise Reflection:

- What did I learn from the quote I chose? If I did this exercise with others, how did the quotes they chose lead me to greater understanding of suspending certainty?
- How might I live out what I learned from this exercise in my interactions today?

EXERCISE 10: Keep the Conversation Ball in the Air

Purpose: To build default prompts that will keep you suspending certainty and interested in knowing more as you discover new ideas.

Guiding Tips: You do not have to follow a specific order with these prompts, nor do you need to use them all. Determine which are most appropriate for your context and for you.

Directions: When someone shares a point of view different from yours or a thought that startles or surprises you, ask two or three follow-up questions that help you suspend your certainty before sharing your point of view.

Question Prompts

- Tell me more.
- What else?
- What's that like?
- What are you noticing?
- What possibilities do you see?
- What's true for you?
- What's happening for you?
- How would you explain this?
- What is your experience of this?

Post-Exercise Reflection:

- How did this experience feel to me?
- Is it challenging to not add my point of view when I want to?
- Which questions are comfortable for me to ask?
- Which might be my go-tos from now on if I want to keep a conversation going?

As you grow up... "You get better at hearing feedback. Rather than assuming that anyone who criticizes you is either trying to humiliate you or is making a mistake, you accept that maybe it would be an idea to take a few things on board. You start to see that you can listen to a criticism and survive it—without having to put on your armor and deny there was ever a problem."—from *The Book of Life, by the School of Life Collective authors and philosophers* https://bit.ly/3tTtLoK

Chapter Reflection Questions: Suspend Certainty

- In what kind of situations am I most defensive? What are my triggers? How might suspending certainty enable me to feel calmer in those circumstances?
- What is one instance that I can now see when I would have benefited from understanding how to suspend certainty? How might I rewrite that script if I were able to relive it?
- How does suspending certainty help me in my work team?
- How will I remind myself to inquire about others' thoughts before advocating my own position?
- In what parts of my work do I need to shift even more into a learner role?
- In what ways do I need to "interrupt" my way of doing things and learn a bit more?

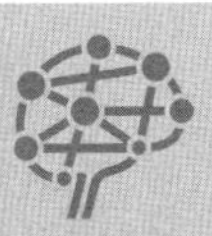

At the time of this publication, there are 7.8 billion people on Earth. If that doesn't make you question your point of view, what will? Yours is one perspective in a very big world.

As you grow up... "You learn that—remarkably—you do sometimes get things wrong. With huge courage, you take your first faltering steps towards (once in a while) apologizing."

—from *The Book of Life, by the School of Life Collective authors and philosophers*

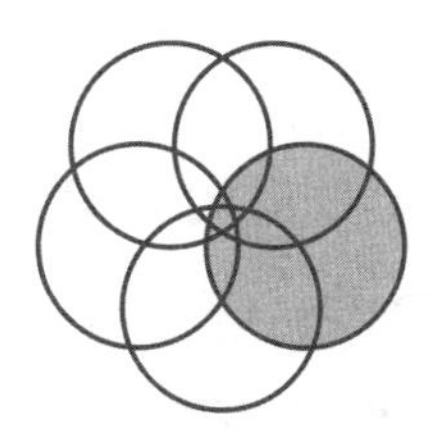

CHAPTER THREE
Facet #3 - Take Responsibility

Most people do not really want freedom, because freedom involves responsibility, and most people are frightened of responsibility.
—Sigmund Freud, father of psychoanalysis

CHAPTER TAKEAWAYS

As you read, consider these reflective questions and make notes of your takeaways.

- Which ideas in this chapter resonate the most with me?
- What seems most worthy of my time?
- Which concepts from this chapter have been the most meaningful and stand out for me?

Guiding Questions

- What are my responsibilities in my role at work?
- What is something I need to take more responsibility for in my work? Consider not just your job description but also your choice of language, how you communicate, your interactions with others, etc.
- How much job-crafting do I do within the boundaries of my job?
- Do I feel in charge of my career? How do I take responsibility for developing myself within my current role and for other future roles I might take?
- Do I feel responsible to contributing to the growth of my profession? If so, how do I exhibit that sense of responsibility?

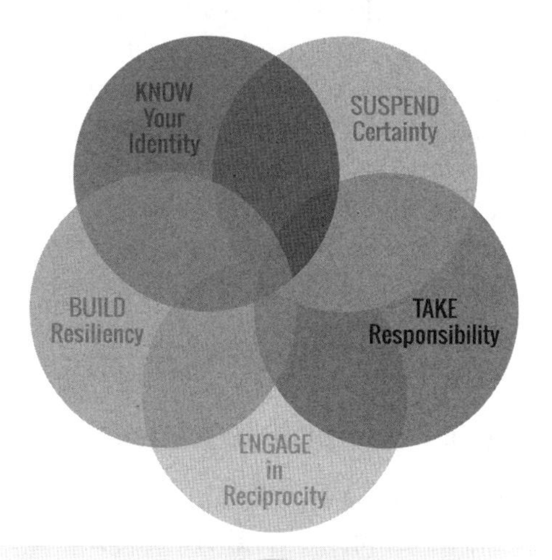

Definition: Taking Responsibility

The power of taking ownership for one's actions and participating in all interactions (with oneself and others) directly, humanely, and productively.

Facet #3: Take Responsibility Definition		
What It Is	**Why It Matters**	**What It Looks/Sounds Like**
Taking ownership for your part of a work product. Owning your language and behavior during interactions with yourself and others. Working as a partner and collaborative teammate in solution-focused conversations. Taking ownership of your personal and professional development. Honoring a commitment to developing one's profession and field of work.	Integral to the organizational health of a workplace and to being an effective colleague and productive team and community member. Strengthens the group as an individual answerable and accountable for what is within their power, including choice of language, behaviors, actions, and communications. Supporting the profession and leaving it better than one found it acknowledges the important work of the field.	Sharing requests, decisions, concerns, disappointments, and grievances in productive ways. Speaking with care and candor to those below, equivalent to, and above on the organizational chart and using solution-oriented mindsets and language. Sharing feedback and apologies with others in authentic ways. Acknowledging others who make a positive difference in your work. Crafting a professional development map for yourself based on your needs in the workplace and hopes for your career.

Take Responsibility: Key Concepts

When we go to work, we know we have obligations and responsibilities for specific tasks. We understand we are accountable for our tasks and work product—what might be called "doing your job." Beyond the "what" of your work and for what you are accountable, in terms of contracts and job descriptions, you are responsible for "how" you do your work. Sometimes it can be described it terms of degree of performance—from "getting by" to "going the extra mile." From simply following the *letter* of the law to going above and beyond and following the *spirit* of the law. Taking responsibility for your work extends to how you choose to contribute to your teams and to the field. How you handle your emotions, how you respond to others, and how you express yourself in various forms of communication are all pieces in your scope and purview—your responsibility. Supervision, evaluation, and the tasks of accountability are done by someone external to you—that's an outside job. Taking responsibility is more of an inside job related to reliability and also a strong awareness of how to positively contribute to the team, a commitment to personal and professional development, and a deep dedication to a high level of work.

Take Responsibility: Dimensions

BE 100% RESPONSIBLE FOR YOUR RESPONSES

Many think of working within a sphere of control. Checking off tasks on a to-do list or sticking to your job description. Yet there is so much more within your sphere of control for which you are responsible. Specifically, you are 100% responsible for how you respond to others, both verbally and through actions. Your responsibility includes how you ask questions, how you share disappointments, and how you share concerns. 100% of what you say is your responsibility.

You have agency over how you provide growth-producing feedback, how you apologize, how you communicate about emotional topics, and how you productively communicate with those above you in the hierarchy. Communications in all these situations are yours to craft. Asking, "How might I communicate my perspective humanely in a kind, supportive, and non-aggressive manner?" is a collective responsibility for us all.

OWN YOUR NEED TO IMPROVE

Zen master Shunryū Suzuki said, "Each of you is perfect the way you are, and you could use a little improvement." You are responsible to your workplace and to your profession. As a lifelong learner, the commitment to disrupt your way of thinking and to seek perspectives beyond your current frames of reference is an expectation. Your responsibilities include stretching yourself and asking, "What do I have responsibility to learn more about?" For example, a board strategic plan initiative may push you into growing your skill set around a given set of strategies or curricula. Or you may be pulled toward personal growth as you recognize a gap between what you know and what you want to know about your subject or your ability to support students. You work within a system and you have our own career trajectory. Learning in both realms is necessary. Thoughts such as, "I am retiring soon, so why bother?" don't align with developing this facet. Learning is continual, and you are a work in progress.

Yet, we don't want to forget the first part of Suzuki's quote, "Each of you is perfect the way you are." So isn't it right to be proud of yourself? Isn't it okay to toot your horn at times? To self-advocate? The answer is, "Yes, and." You should recognize your strengths and share your knowledge and you need to stretch, reflect, and refine your craft. Your workplace reflects society, and past learning may not always be enough as challenges arise and changes happen. If we do not evolve and adapt, we succumb to entropy. We are not able to do what's right for our communities. If we don't learn about supporting students more effectively by creating a safe environment and using culturally responsive practices we are guilty of professional malpractice. So yes, share your knowledge and do so without shame. And, yet with pride also have humility. Promote yourself and also live up to the top of your job description. Model that you proving yourself is always improving yourself.

SPEAK UP THOUGHTFULLY

Public service announcements aren't just for airports. When you see a change that could be helpful in a situation, speak up. Are you asked for feedback? Offer productive thoughts. What would be helpful for others to know, and how might you say what you want to in a way that someone will hear it and not be dismissive? Make your words productive, solution-oriented, and humane. Do you notice the group isn't hearing from everyone? Name it humanely. Do you recognize that you might have overstepped? Apologize. The two parts of this facet—speaking up and speaking up thoughtfully—are inextricably intertwined. Work on your ability to speak up—and to speak up with respect, tact, and consideration.

GO BEYOND YOURSELF AND GROW YOUR PROFESSION

Every profession continually grows and changes. Your work is to help in that growth. Joining and supporting professional organizations, developing and becoming part of networks, and sitting on committees are important additions to your individual learning. Consider it a responsibility to support someone else's development—mentor, coach, build the pipeline for those who will take your place. When you see the bigger picture of your profession, the system's needs come into view. You can help others and help your profession grow. Succession planning is a key element of leadership. In addition, we have a collective responsibility to leave the field better than when we came into it. Personally, I have worked with those coming into my profession in graduate school programs; become a coach to those new to my district; volunteered to present at local, state, and national conferences; and written for journals in my field. It's critical that we contribute to the field rather than just our school.

DIMENSIONS—TAKE RESPONSIBILITY

Be 100% Responsible for Your Responses

Own Your Need to Improve

Speak Up... Thoughtfully

Go Beyond Yourself and Grow the Profession

Facet #3: Take Responsibility Characteristics & Continuum

Characteristics	Stage 1	Stage 2	Stage 3
Is solution focused in sharing contributions with the team. Has the linguistic skills to contribute feedback effectively to the team.	I am aware of the difference between complaining or blaming and problem solving. I do not always have the skill set (linguistic/emotional) to make the switch to being a problem solver and solution-focused contributor. I'm not always able to manage my responses when I am anxious.	I understand that we all need to see ourselves as change agents in our workplaces, and I move past complaining to problem solving. I consciously work on my ability to offer humane feedback.	I ask myself and others about challenges I see in a situation, am easily able to name them humanely, and skillfully find productive ways to move forward.
Recognizes limits of strategies, learning theories, and leadership beliefs. Takes responsibility to seek out new learning.	I have a surface understanding that my current actions might not work best now or in the future, but I don't immediately make changes. I recognize that new learning and a change is a good thing—in theory.	I know and can articulate what it looks like to be good at my job what leadership looks like. I know the limits of my individual style, strategies, and beliefs, and I take action to learn more. Putting this into practice is something I do inconsistently.	I know and can articulate various strategies for working and leading, as well as different learning theories. I know and can articulate which strategies, theories, and styles I use in my work, and I can recognize and appreciate which strategies, theories, and styles others choose. I routinely find ways to advance my own learning and consistently put my new learning into practice.

Facet #3: Take Responsibility Characteristics & Continuum

Characteristics	Stage 1	Stage 2	Stage 3
Engages comfortably in conflict; takes a stand humanely.	I am aware that conflict exists. I am not confident that I can find the right words during challenging interactions. I fear that negative feelings will overwhelm me. I ask a supervisor to manage uncomfortable situations instead of taking them on myself.	I take responsibility for productive interactions in challenging moments. I build my emotional and linguistic savvy to speak respectfully when I see violated boundaries violated or broken group norms.	I know conflict is will occur, and I am comfortable surfacing challenging topics in order to explore what is hidden. I take full responsibility for managing my emotional responses, and I actively work to improve my ability to remain resourceful in moments of tension.
Recognizes each team member as responsible for their individual contributions to the team and its effectiveness. Is mindful of being a citizen of the organization responsible for its health.	I am just beginning to understand my responsibility to hold myself accountable for how I act, how I respond, and how I contribute positively to the collective.	I question others in order to move to the group toward owning and solving problems and to shift the group away from blame. I learn skills to hold others accountable by focusing on requests rather than complaints, and I speak up when I see something unsound, unsafe, or emotionally damaging to others.	I easily take responsibility for myself—my language, actions, and contributions. I seek to influence my work teams positively. I extend and create space for each team member to have ownership.
Acknowledges others' contributions and apologizes when wrong.	I'm aware that I am responsible for acknowledging and praising others, and apologizing when needed. I often do not remember to take these actions.	I am learning to acknowledge and give positive, constructive feedback to others. I apologize when needed, although awkwardly.	I am aware of my responsibility to offer positive and well-constructed feedback to others, and I regularly do so. I offer timely and effective apologies.
Seeks out improvement opportunities. Takes responsibility for individual growth and development.	I attend professional learning when it is mandated and offered. I attend staff meetings/ team meetings.	I seek out additional learning opportunities beyond those mandated or scheduled, and I take advantage of opportunities that further my career goals. I take courses or attend institutes, conferences, Twitter chats, and so on.	I know that it is my responsibility to grow, learn, and develop. I intentionally seek learning opportunities that challenge and support my development outside my comfort zone.
Takes responsibility for not only individual growth and development in areas of interest and in the interest of the organization, but also committed in growth of the profession as a whole.	I contribute to my team and workplace.	I take responsibility for informal mentoring, leading professional learning, volunteering for a professional organization conference, etc.	I consider it my professional responsibility to give back, and I formally lead events/ studies/coaching. I work on succession planning and think about my legacy.

Take Responsibility: Self-Assessment

Another way to look at taking responsibility is by self-assessing behaviors that align with its related characteristics. What might you do or say if you were progressing through the stages of developing awareness around taking responsibility? For each statement, select the response that most represents where you feel you are.

- When I hear someone complaining, I acknowledge the person's feelings and then work to move the conversation to solutions.
  - ☐ I haven't thought about it.
  - ☐ I have given this some thought, and I'm getting better at this.
  - ☐ I have given this a lot of thought, and I am very good at this.
- I use language that encourages the group to seek solutions rather than blame. Instead of saying, "But that won't work," I make a point of staying outcome-focused and saying something like, "Well, what might work?"
  - ☐ I haven't thought about it.
  - ☐ I have given this some thought, and I'm getting better at this.
  - ☐ I have given this a lot of thought, and I am very good at this.
- I try to address my frustrations professionally so my input has a better chance of being taken seriously.
  - ☐ I haven't thought about it.
  - ☐ I have given this some thought, and I'm getting better at this.
  - ☐ I have given this a lot of thought, and I am very good at this.
- After talking to others or thinking about what could work better; I take next steps and help others make changes.
  - ☐ I haven't thought about it.
  - ☐ I have given this some thought, and I'm getting better at this.
  - ☐ I have given this a lot of thought, and I am very good at this.
- When I'm asked to take on a task, participate in a project, or help roll out an initiative, I easily ask for clarification or assistance when I don't understand what to do.
  - ☐ I haven't thought about it.
  - ☐ I have given this some thought, and I'm getting better at this.
  - ☐ I have given this a lot of thought, and I am very good at this.
- I know apologizing is often awkward, but I do it and feel good that I did.
  - ☐ I haven't thought about it.
  - ☐ I have given this some thought, and I'm getting better at this.
  - ☐ I have given this a lot of thought, and I am very good at this.
- I recognize that I control how I speak to others, however challenging a situation, and I use humane and growth-producing conversation techniques.
  - ☐ I haven't thought about it.
  - ☐ I have given this some thought, and I'm getting better at this.
  - ☐ I have given this a lot of thought, and I am very good at this.

- I recognize that I am a part of a collective/team/department, and I'm responsible for helping to increase the group's positivity.
  - ☐ I haven't thought about it.
  - ☐ I have given this some thought, and I'm getting better at this.
  - ☐ I have given this a lot of thought, and I am very good at this.
- I recognize that I am responsible for building my persuasion skills to avoid feeling frustrated when others don't see my point of view.
  - ☐ I haven't thought about it.
  - ☐ I have given this some thought, and I'm getting better at this.
  - ☐ I have given this a lot of thought, and I am very good at this.
- I recognize that as a professional, I do not know enough. I seek out professional learning to help me be more successful and keep up with what's happening in my field to help further my profession.
  - ☐ I haven't thought about it.
  - ☐ I have given this some thought, and I'm getting better at this.
  - ☐ I have given this a lot of thought, and I am very good at this.
- I can respectfully share my perspective with someone who says something emotionally insensitive or disrespectful about another person or a group of people.
  - ☐ I haven't thought about it.
  - ☐ I have given this some thought, and I'm getting better at this.
  - ☐ I have given this a lot of thought, and I am very good at this.
- I am working on my semantic sensitivity and take responsibility for my language and tone in regards to how I come across to others.
  - ☐ I haven't thought about it.
  - ☐ I have given this some thought, and I'm getting better at this.
  - ☐ I have given this a lot of thought, and I am very good at this.
- I share my knowledge when I think it would help the team without sounding conceited.
  - ☐ I haven't thought about it.
  - ☐ I have given this some thought, and I'm getting better at this.
  - ☐ I have given this a lot of thought, and I am very good at this.
- I am clear about what I want to learn each year as part of my professional growth, and I set goals.
  - ☐ I haven't thought about it.
  - ☐ I have given this some thought and I'm getting better at this.
  - ☐ I have given this a lot of thought, and I am very good at this.

Now that you have selected your responses:

Look. Look for patterns. Where are you most aware/least aware?

Reflect. Which statements surprise you and merit future thought and attention?

Consider. How might learning more about yourself in response to these statements support your development and assist you in your work?

Take Responsibility: Self-Talk by Stages

Another way to look at the characteristics of this facet is to experience what self-talk might look like at each stage. What might you say to yourself or to others at each stage of taking responsibility?

Facet #3: Take Responsibility Self-Talk by Stages

	Stage 1	Stage 2	Stage 3
What am I saying to myself?	"Wow, that was a bit hurtful. I hope someone says something." "Yikes, I feel bad about something I said, but I don't know how to apologize." "I think I will share my thoughts with my colleagues when I get a chance in private but not here." "I feel on the spot when someone asks my opinion. I just don't have the right words quickly." "Someone will tell me what I am supposed to be doing." "I'm second guessing myself. What might others say about this? What might my supervisor think? I better check."	"I am trying to speak up when something hurtful is said. Why don't others speak up, too?" "I get it. I gotta apologize. So awkward." "Yup, blaming and venting isn't going to help the situation, but how to change that?" "I think I have some good ideas. My contributions will be useful to the group's next steps." "This meeting could be going better. How could I help move it along more positively?" "I did my homework, and I hope everyone did."	"I am very aware that I am in charge of me. It's on me to speak up when we see something professionally unsound or emotionally unsafe." "I will clean up what I mess up." "When whining gets the best of me, I gotta refocus on solutions." "What might be the most supportive way to say what I want to say?" "I am up for it. Happy to help." "I co-created the meeting outcomes and am up for being present at this time."
What am I saying to others?	"If I sometimes sound like I am complaining rather than sharing concerns, would you gently mention something to me, please?" "Feedback stings so just a few pieces at a time, please." "I really struggle to speak up. I shut down when I am hurt or I don't understand." "I feel like I would be willing to help out our profession more if the group were doing it, too."	"I am trying, but I fumble over the right words. But I am trying, and I need to not beat myself up since I am a work in progress." "That learning opportunity sounds interesting. Send me more information, please." "I see that feedback is useful, and I work hard to better give and accept it." "I understand that hurt and confusion are emotions, and I can separate myself from them so I can see the learning." "I would try being a mentor if someone asked me."	"What can I do to help?" "Growth is a constant. So let's dive in." "I can accept feedback without feeling defensive, and I am willing to offer positive, constructive feedback in helpful ways." "I am aware when I get hooked by an emotional reaction and I try to course correct." "I am getting much better at sharing my thoughts in a healthy, productive manner." "It is my responsibility to grow my profession. I am always ready to support others on their growth journeys."

Take Responsibility: Exercises for Development

All of these exercises align with the parts of the continuum and the self-assessment in one way or another. There is no specific sequence for these exercises. All thinking and reflection is good.

Remember:

- These are intentionally called exercises, in contrast to activities. The goal is to develop in this facet. This type of growth doesn't always feel good or easy.
- You can decide which exercises align with your specific focus within the continuum for this facet. You can do some of the exercises—or you can do them all. Self-determination rules.
- There is no expectation that the exercises be done perfectly; there is no perfect score.
- There is no time limit on how long an exercise should take.

EXERCISE 1: A Dialogue with Dissatisfaction and Responsibility

Purpose: To creatively explore your relationship with the ideas of dissatisfaction and responsibility.

Guiding Tips: Allow this conceit to work. Pretend you actually can talk to these concepts as people. Try to improvise and see what comes up. Believing this exercise is too silly will not help the work. If you become interested in working more with anthropomorphizing feelings, read *The Book of Qualities* by J. Ruth Gendler.

Directions: Imagine that Dissatisfaction and Responsibility are two real people with whom you are now beginning a conversation. In a journal, start a dialogue with them. Pose a question to Dissatisfaction or to Responsibility and see how each responds. For example, you might begin like this.

You: Dissatisfaction, I often wonder why I think you're fun to hang out with. Why do you think I feel that way about you?

Dissatisfaction: I'm the fun one at the party. We go to the kitchen and dish the dirt. I love juicy gossip and venting and complaining. I'm easy to get along with, unlike that sourpuss, Responsibility.

You: Yeah, Responsibility. I think you are a total downer. You're the person who makes me make my bed and floss and take ownership of my life. You're no fun. How do you see yourself?

Responsibility: I'm a lot to handle at times. Acknowledging that you know me might make you nervous because you think you have to be perfect and I will blame you if you don't do things the "right" way. You often seem more concerned with what others think instead of recognizing that understanding me is freeing. I can help you feel like you're more of an adult, rather than feeling beneath someone else or living how someone else wants you to. You'll own your life choices.

Possible question stems to ask Dissatisfaction or Responsibility

How do you manage...?

What do you think of...?

What are your expectations of...?

How might I...?

What would you say to me if I said...?

Post-Exercise Refection:

- What did I learn about my relationship with Dissatisfaction and with Responsibility?
- Do I see these two seemingly opposing forces having any chance to "work it out?"
- What questions am I left with?
- With whom am I comfortable having a conversation about my beliefs or worries?

EXERCISE 2: Plan Instead of Gripe

Purpose: To move from complaining to active problem solving. From a place of victimhood to a place of ownership and possibility. Robert Garmston and Bruce Wellman suggest in *The Adaptive School: A Sourcebook for Developing Collaborative Groups* that you ask yourself two questions when you want to complain: "What do I want to happen instead of what is happening?" and "What can I request or propose to make that happen?" The answers to these questions can move you from griping to planning.

Guiding Tips: Give yourself time to complete the questions. You may get stuck on the first section and want to quit the exercise. That feeling is normal. Many of us are not accustomed to thinking proactively *and* planning for desired outcomes. Be gentle with yourself.

Directions: Think about an issue, a person, a project, or an assignment you feel unhappy with—something or someone that feels difficult and you just want off your plate. When you want to complain, follow the following steps in the order below. Do not skip around. This exercise won't take a problem away, but can help change your outlook and give you a scaffold for writing out a more proactive communication you can share.

1. State the problem succinctly. What is the presenting issue? What is going on that you don't think is working/helpful? Can you clearly frame the problem? Could you put it in a 25-word telegram or a 280-character tweet? Is it possible that something else might surface that is a root cause of the problem you've identified? That is okay. You do want to try to localize the problem, so don't make it too general. And try to frame it in language that doesn't sting.

   ____

   ____

   ____

2. Describe what you want instead. The problem might not go away, but this step asks you to consider a more positive future state. You may find that you have a desire to stay with step one and that focusing on the drama is exciting. Sometimes there's seems to be more satisfaction in complaining. But ask yourself what it would look like if the problem was gone. Stay future focused with your answers.

___

___

___

___

3. Detail what behaviors or specific actions you'd like to see if the problem were solved. At this step, pay attention to details. Broad goals such as "have better communication with that colleague" or "garner greater respect from that student" do not yet have enough detail to help envision the future. What might "better communication"' or "more respect" look or sound like? What actions could a person take that would show you they are "taking initiative?" How would a colleague behave to demonstrate they are more interested in communicating well? Try to write down at least three or four specific behaviors that could demonstrate what you want. Getting clear about desired behaviors takes time, but it's worth the effort.

___

___

___

___

4. Now step back. Ask yourself, "As I write this, does it sound like I am expressing a complaint or expressing a concern? If I were the person hearing from someone else what it would look like if the problem was gone, would what they are requesting or suggesting sound doable?"

___

___

___

___

TALKING TO DAD

In this video Jennifer recalls having a hard conversation with her dad about her concerns with his eyesight and his driving. Listen in as she describes how she handled this uncomfortable situation.

https://bit.ly/3daaQyS

Post-Exercise Refection:

- How do I feel after figuring out a proactive approach to the problem?
- Some say these steps decrease the drama in a situation and increase a sense of resourcefulness. Do I agree?
- Which step was hardest? Why?
- In which situations might these four steps be helpful?

EXERCISE 3: Building On Instead of Yeah-Butting

(based on *Conversation Transformation: Recognize and Overcome the 6 Most Destructive Communication Patterns*)

Purpose: To communicate more effectively in collaborative situations with those who dismiss ideas by saying suggestions will not work (yeah-but people). While yeah-butting is frustrating, your responsibility in this exercise is to learn to stay engaged. You are developing skills to keep a conversation going so you can examine issues more closely.

Guiding Tips: Keep in mind a person dismissing ideas is always at least 10% right. Ask yourself, "How could I be wrong?" as you work with those who dismiss your ideas. Stay humble.

Directions:

1. Think of a real situation in your life or work where your opinion conflicted with someone else's idea of a next step or next action and they rejected your suggestion as undoable.

2. Find three ways to agree with the yeah-but and *then* add a comment or question incorporating your concern.

Example 1: A person on your team complains that a project wasn't brought to his attention early enough and suggests that the group doesn't know enough to finish it successfully. He says things like, "We could, but we..." and "Had we done this, but we didn't..." The project is nonnegotiable and the group is moving ahead.

You might say: You're right that this should have been more clearly discussed with us earlier (agreement #1). You also have a point that the time frame in which we are asked to do this is limited (agreement #2). Also, I agree that it might not be as successful as we hoped (agreement #3). And given this isn't going off our plate, what do you think is our next best step to move ahead with this work? (question).

Example 2: A colleague is unhappy with a new initiative that asks teams to emphasize process as well as product. Group members are asked to take time for check-ins and inquire about one another's psychological health. The unhappy person does not have much experience in this area and now must lead their group. Their reaction is, "But this isn't part of my role," and "But I barely have enough time to do what I need to."

You might say: "I agree with you that this shifts our focus a bit to emphasize the social emotional side of our work interactions (agreement #1). And I agree that isn't everyone's strong suit (agreement #2). And I agree that it is going to take us a little time to figure out how to do this (agreement #3). How might we approach learning this skill more effectively and efficiently to keep both product *and* process front and center? (question).

Example 3: A colleague is unhappy because the group is working remotely. They are an extrovert, and having to do much of the work on their own doesn't align with their preferred work style.

You might say: "You're right. This way of working is difficult because you can't be with others in person (agreement #1). And while I agree it's not optimal, you do have access to me and the support of the team when you need it (agreement #2). And I know you understand that our safety is behind this choice (agreement # 3). So what do think we should do next so we can move forward? Would you like to schedule some video meetings so we can talk it through? (question).

Post-Exercise Reflection:

- What was challenging about this agree-then-question exercise? How might this shift my conversations in the future?
- How might I use this technique? In which situations might this be useful?

Once you've articulated (the other person's) perspective for them, they feel understood. And a person who feels understood is getting a feel-good wave of chemicals in their brain. The one you are really going for is oxytocin, the bonding chemical. Once they get a hit of oxytocin, everything is going to change. They'll feel bonded to you.

—Chris Voss, former lead FBI hostage negotiator

EXERCISE 4: Give Growth-Producing Feedback to Superiors

Purpose: To share growth producing feedback with supervisors. We can be mindful of roles and balance that with our responsibility to work effectively with *all* our colleagues, including those in positions of authority. Learning to give feedback "up" is a key skill to develop in terms of taking responsibility.

Guiding Tips: Know your context. Some supervisors may gather input once a year on an anonymous staff survey, and sharing feedback more often or face-to-face could be unusual. Other supervisors might have an open-door policy and frequently receive unsolicited input. Be aware of individuals' comfort levels, status concerns, language, and of how commonplace or outside the norm it is for your supervisor to receive feedback. You might think, "I can't tell my supervisor what to do." You aren't telling them what to do. You are offering suggestions.

Directions: As you plan to offer input to your supervisor, use the map from Exercise 2: Plan Instead of Gripe and shape the language you will use to share information.

1. Be other-focused rather than self-focused in your wording. Instead of saying, "I need to tell you what I am feeling," or "We need to talk about how things are going in my department," ask a starting question to get permission to offer feedback. Make this inquiry before offering the feedback you prepared.

Here are a few questions:

- "Are you open to hearing a few ideas or additional techniques?"
- "Would you be interested in some thoughts about increasing your influence with more of the staff?"

The idea of asking for permission before offering your thoughts and suggestions indicates to the supervisor that you want them to be successful and you and your colleagues want to be successful, too. You're saying, "This input is offered with the intention of helping us all be even more effective."

2. If your supervisor says now isn't a good time, be prepared to let the matter go for now. Wait a few days or a week. If you truly feel it is important, you might return and say, "Is this a better time to talk?" or "Are you open to revisiting the question I asked you last week?" or "I'm wondering if this is a better time to share some ideas?" Again, you are asking permission.
3. Have the conversation in the supervisor's office if possible as they may feel more psychologically safe there.
4. If you are uncomfortable sharing input or suggestions alone, go with a colleague. Be mindful that the supervisor may feel "ganged up on" if there is a large group.
5. Offer your ideas in the form of suggestions, considerations, or recommendations using Exercise 2: Plan Instead of Gripe. You are not making demands. Presenting a supervisor with an expectation or demand most likely won't work. Power dynamics will come out. Using words including *options, possible ideas, hunches,* and *suggestions* or phrases such as *considerations for what to do next* or *recommendations as we move forward*

allows your supervisor the ultimate choice for next steps. Communication consultants Laura Lipton and Bruce Wellman suggest a "Give Three" approach. Offering someone one suggestion doesn't give them a choice, other than accepting or rejecting that idea. Offering two suggestions may limit the listener's thinking and they might choose the second alternative or whichever one you tonally emphasized. Giving three suggestions, and *truly* making them suggestions, offers the listener a real choice. Have three suggestions at the ready.

6. Be prepared to have your supervisor ask you to meet them halfway and for you take a few next steps on your end. Be ready to say yes or no. If you say no, offer reasons rather than excuses. Most administrators appreciate having others as part of a solution, so offering to take on a task is a good next step.

Post-Exercise Reflection:

- What was the most challenging part of trying to give feedback to a supervisor?
- What was most satisfying?

After you try to offer feedback, use the interaction as the basis to complete Exercise 5: Post-Action Review.

EXERCISE 5: Post-Action Review

Purpose: To develop an ability to consider responses after an experience. These questions, if asked regularly, create a habitual way of thinking about your practice and living out one of Maya Angelou's edicts: "I did then what I knew how to do. Now that I know better, I do better."

Guiding Tips: This review can be done by yourself or with colleague.

Directions: Identify a lesson, a presentation, a completed project, a just-finished conversation or finished piece of work for which you would like to determine the plusses and minuses. Talk through and/or take notes on your answers to the questions. The idea of reflecting is directly aligned with "taking responsibility" especially through making decisions to move forward with more intention (know better, do better).

- What was successful? What worked? How do you know it worked?

  ____

  ____

  ____

- What did you learn? What do you think others learned? How do you know that they learned?

  ____

  ____

  ____

- What challenges or concerns do you have?

____

____

____

- Can you think of another way you could have approached the issue? What effect might that have had?

____

____

____

- What linguistic decisions did you make that helped others move forward?

____

____

____

- Is there anything you could or would do differently next time?

____

____

____

- How would you describe your progress toward meeting your goal?

____

____

____

- What actions do you need to take in order to move forward?

____

____

____

- What human and material resources can support you as you move forward?

____

____

____

Post-Exercise Reflection:

- How can I incorporate this kind of post-action review more seamlessly into my work and learning experiences?
- How can I shorten this list to two to three questions to make it easier to take responsibility for changes/next steps?

EXERCISE 6: Learn How to Apologize

(based on *On Apology* by Aaron Lazare)

Purpose: To learn a scaffold for writing an apology when we are defensive, make hurtful comments, overstep, are rude, or make a mistake.

Guiding Tips: Be clear about what you are apologizing for. For example, you can apologize for how you said something without apologizing for what you said. Apologizing is an important skill and is for moments that you truly feel regret for something you said or did and you seek an adult way to acknowledge your misstep.

Directions: Consider a particular moment or experience for which you wish to apologize for your language, actions, inactions, etc. Follow the steps to write an apology.

- Identify the person or persons to whom you owe an apology.
- Acknowledge the offending behavior in detail.
- Recognize the impact the behavior may have had on the person.
- Acknowledge that the misstep or action violated a social and/or moral contract/norm with others in your community, team, etc.
- Express your remorse sincerely.
- Express your wish to reclaim the person's trust.
- Make reparations. Offer to do something, buy something, change something.

Two sample apologies:

> Dear Maria,
>
> I'm sorry for cutting you off in our meeting today. I snapped and didn't allow you to continue with your idea for helping Mathias. My behavior was disrespectful. My reasons for acting inappropriately don't matter. What matters is that I messed up, I feel bad, and I will not cut you off again. I'm sorry.
>
> Best,
Me
>
> Dear Tom,
>
> I want to apologize for not responding to your queries via email this past week. I did receive the emails and saw the deadline you offered, and I didn't meet it. My inaction caused a backup for the proposal and delayed the next steps that you and the team needed to take. I offer this apology as an acknowledgment that I am aware I didn't follow through on our agreement. I am sending this email with the promise that I will do all I can to follow through and meet deadlines with our next project.
>
> Best,
Me

Post-Exercise Reflection:

- What seems easy or difficult about the steps to making a complete apology?
- When I communicate an apology, do I usually use a similar structure?
- Which parts of the scaffold are new to me?
- What am I discovering about my work and language choices in this facet?

WAYS TO BOTCH AN APOLOGY (FROM *ON APOLOGY* BY AARON LAZARE)

- **Offer a vague and/or incomplete acknowledgment.** Say, "I am sorry," with no elaboration.
- **Use the passive voice.** Say, "Mistakes were made," or "We made a terrible mistake."
- **Make the offense conditional.** Say, "If mistakes were made, then I am sorry." Let go of "ifs."
- **Question whether the victim was harmed.** Say, "If anyone was hurt," or "If you were offended." This kind of statements implies that the person may not have been hurt, and you're apologizing only out of your own generosity.
- **Minimize the offense.** Say something like, "In the grand scheme of things, this really isn't a big deal."
- **Over use the word *sorry*.** Emphasizing the word "sorry" too strongly or using a patronizing tone communicates condescension.
- **Apologize for the wrong offense.** Say, "I am sorry you feel bad."
- **Apologize to the wrong party.** Apologizing in general to your group rather than reconciling with the individual who was hurt is manipulating the apology to protect yourself.
- **Apologize for the wrong thing.** Say, "I'm sorry for the embarrassment I caused." Instead, say you are sorry for what you did to cause the embarrassment.

It's appropriate to apologize if you express your anger in a way that has taken someone's dignity away, but apologizing because you expressed your opinions, ideas, or feelings of anger takes away your dignity.

—Rosalind Wiseman

EXERCISE 7: Asking for Help

Purpose: To build your ability to ask for help in productive ways. In the book *Embarrassment: And the Emotional Underlife of Learning*, Thomas Newkirk says we may feel "doubly incompetent" when we can't articulate how and when we are stuck. Students in writing classes find it challenging to ask for help. Newkirk says: "They have trouble with their writing, and trouble saying what the trouble is." This exercise is to assist you with finding the language you need to ask for assistance.

Guiding Tips: This exercise is designed to help you ask for assistance more effectively and gain insight in order to take next steps. This is *not* about someone else solving a problem for you. The responsibility remains with you to follow through. Remember to choose language that will not irritate the person you are asking for help. Comments that push responsibility, such as "You need to help me with this" or "It's your job to help me" aren't useful. Do not let feelings of frustration move you to into a complaining space. This exercise helps you learn to take responsibility for gathering information in a fruitful way.

Directions: Think about an assignment you have or a task you need clarity around. You have a right to seek out guidance in a professional manner for any aspect of any task or assignment you do not fully understand. Decide what you need to know and see if any of the sentence stems below align with the clarification you need.

- "In order for me to do this work well, I have these questions..."
- Can you give me more information about what I will be doing?
- Will I get training or tutorials about how to do the work?
- Can you explain more about why this is the way we are going?
- As the work is rolling out, I see I need to spend additional time on this. Do you see other work that I could take off my plate or put to the side for the time being?
- What's my timeline for getting this up and running?
- What will happen if I am not successful?

Post-Exercise Reflection:

Ask yourself:

- How did the questioning go?
- Did I receive answers that support my efforts?
- What else am I uncertain about that I also need to ask?
- How might I formulate those additional question(s)?

NOT GONNA STEAL YOUR GAINS

In this video, Jennifer recalls a story from a weight lifting experience with a spotter at the gym.

https://bit.ly/3fdCDRP

COMPLAINING TO MY BOSS

Jennifer describes a meeting with a former superintendent in which she complained about her situation. Watch the video to learn how her superintendent responded.

https://bit.ly/3smAFCr

There are moments in life when keeping silent becomes a fault and speaking an obligation. A civic duty, a moral challenge, a categorical imperative from which we cannot escape.

—Oriana Fallaci, Italian journalist

"In order for help seeking to be both effective and instrumental, the individual must know enough to know what is not known, to know what could be known, and to have some reasonable ideas about where and how such knowledge might be gained."—Sharon Nelson-Le Gall

---

EXERCISE 8: Take Ownership of Your Own Professional Development and Contributions to Your Field

Purpose: To create a personal professional development plan around *your* hopes and dreams as you take responsibility for your career. To review the opportunities you have to contribute to your field.

Guiding Tips: Brainstorm ideas with someone within your field or department who knows about opportunities, organizations, or networks that align with your goals. Look through your networks on Facebook, Twitter, or Instagram to find communities that can help you locate personal learning opportunities that meet your needs and assist others to learn and grow within your field.

Directions: Complete the tasks below.

1. Find a job description or design one. Rewrite it into a skill, capacity, mindset self-assessment. It could include the standards and responsibilities for your job, the standards and skills needed for a role you aspire to, or a job description for a role you hope to have in a few years.

2. Once you have listed a set of skills, identify the foci for your professional learning. You could choose one or up to five skills. Don't say "all of the above." Make the plan actionable and timely.

3. Write down your professional growth goal(s). What are the next steps for your development? How would you describe your goals to someone? How do the goals relate to your professional aspirations? By focusing on your goals, what do you hope to be able to do that you can't do now?

4. Consider how you might contribute to your field. Where do you have expertise? How could you share that with others? What needed skills do you have? Where and how might those skills be used?

5. Determine your next steps. What activities could you engage in in order to obtain new skills? What activities could positively affect your job performance or ready you for your next job? Consider your next best step to add your voice and skills to your field.

Goals might include: (adapted from The Institute for Education Leadership (IEL), Ontario, CA, Self-Assessment Tool for Aspiring School Leaders)

- Experience writing in your field.
- Leadership in associations or networks.
- Attendance at regional/national/international conferences.
- Participation in book studies around your goals.

- Participation in action research.
- Getting training in specific communication skills.
- Gaining skills to work with constituencies and stakeholders you'd like to influence.
- Learning about national and global trends in your field.
- Knowledge and understanding of the needs of adults in teams and organizations.
- Facilitating groups, including knowledge about effective teamwork.
- Increasing ability and skill levels to give and receive feedback.
- Skills in conflict management and effective use of conflict.
- Peer coaching.
- Shadowing leaders in your field.
- Mentoring new employees.
- Developing technology skills to support student and adult learning experiences.
- Opportunities to lead professional learning.
- Knowing different roles and responsibilities and explaining career paths to those roles; demonstrating understanding of the system.
- Ability to budget.
- Managing school resources and operations, such as through participation on a school leadership team.
- Participating on an employee hiring committee.
- Developing oral and written skills.

Offerings to the field might include:

- Leadership in associations or networks.
- Participation in action research.
- Lobbying policy makers and advocating for educational reform.
- Mentoring or peer coaching.
- Leading professional learning opportunities, Twitter chats, online workshops.
- Facilitating teams.
- Participating on hiring committees and/or negotiation teams.

6. Start a timeline. When should your next step be? Your second? Your third? What is your timeline for your goal(s)? Would having a support system or coach be beneficial?

Post-Exercise Reflection:

- Do I feel more agency and ownership over my professional future?
- How might I take one step to move toward my goals?
- How can I take next steps to determine how to contribute to my field in ways that are doable and supportive to my community?

EXERCISE 9: Journal with Quotations About Responsibility

Purpose: To see what others have said about responsibility and how you are connected to and challenged by this facet.

Guiding Tips: There is no perfect quote. Pick one that most connects to you in the moment or challenges you at this time.

Directions: Take 5 to 10 minutes to write in your journal in response to the quote you select. What are your a-has (insights), your hmms (ponderings), your ouches (awareness of weakness)?

- "Look at the word responsibility—'response-ability'—the ability to choose your response. Highly proactive people recognize that responsibility. They do not blame the circumstances, conditions or conditioning for their behavior. Their behavior is a product of their own conscious choice, based on values, rather than a product of their conditions, based on feeling."—Stephen R. Covey, American Author
- "When a man points a finger at someone else, he should remember that four of his fingers are pointing at himself."—Louis Nizer, American trial lawyer
- "The time is always right to do what is right."—Martin Luther King Jr., social activist
- "Most people do not really want freedom, because freedom involves responsibility and most people are frightened of responsibility." —Sigmund Freud, father of psychoanalysis
- "When participants enter the room of a learning event knowing full well that they chose to be there, the social contract of their learning has shifted dramatically." —Peter Koestenbaum and Peter Block, authors of *Freedom and Accountability at Work*
- "In dreams begin responsibilities."—W.B. Yeats, Irish poet
- "You cannot escape the responsibility of tomorrow by evading it today." —Abraham Lincoln, US president

Post-Exercise Reflection:

- What did I notice about my quote choice and how I framed my response? What did I learn about myself? If I did this exercise with others, which quotes did they choose?
- How might I live out what I learned from this exercise in my interactions today?

If we began to believe employees are 'walking freedoms,' accountable for creating the world in which they live, it would change many of our ways of dealing with them.

—Peter Koestenbaum and Peter Block, *Freedom and Accountability at Work: Applying Philosophic Insight to the Real World*

Chapter Reflection Questions: Take Responsibility

- Do I do more than the bullet points of my job description? Do I internalize and express my workplace's mission out loud?
- Do I speak up when I need help? When I see a way to improve an outcome?
- Do I take responsibility for apologizing when my impact isn't helpful?
- How might I take more responsibility for my work—at the top or at the edges of my role? What would that mean?
- In what ways can I take charge of my career?
- In what ways do I contribute to my field?

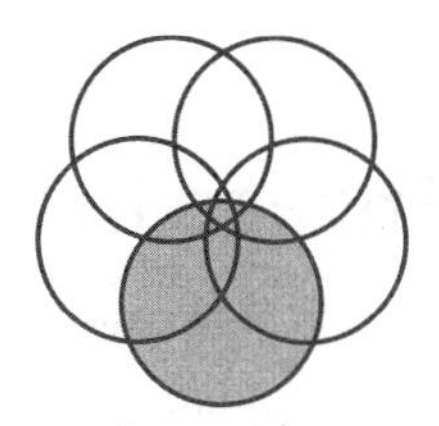

CHAPTER FOUR
Facet #4 - Engage in Reciprocity

Whatever affects one directly, affects all indirectly. I can never be what I ought to be until you are what you ought to be. This is the interrelated structure of reality.

—Martin Luther King Jr., social activist

CHAPTER TAKEAWAYS

As you read, consider these as final reflective questions and make notes as your takeaways.

- Which ideas in this chapter resonate the most with me?
- What has been worthy of my time?
- Which concepts from this chapter have been the most meaningful and stand out for me?

Guiding Questions

- How do I embody the role of an effective group member?
- How do I demonstrate the idea of mutual respect for others through my actions and my words?
- In what ways do I embody the "both/and" work of completing team tasks and building team relationships?
- How does this African proverb resonate in my work life? "If you want to go fast, go alone. If you want to go far, go together." (Note: It is challenging to find this quote attributed to any specific African country or a specific African people but it is found in an approximate phrasing in the Swahili language centering its origin on the African continent.)

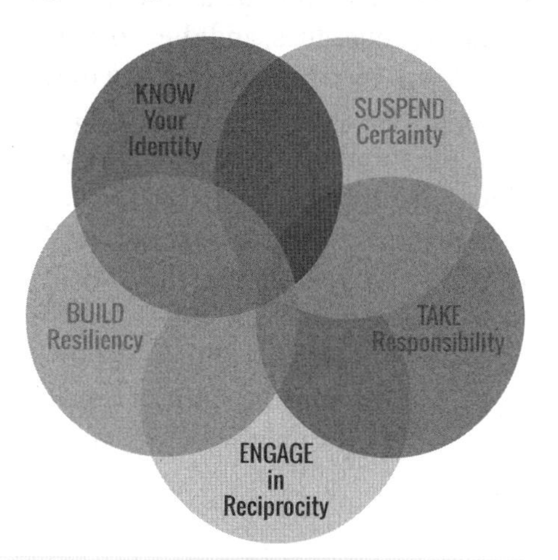

Definition: Engage in Reciprocity

The capability to demonstrate respect for team members and their contributions, for the whole of the organization, and for the collective work of the team and organization.

Facet #4: Engage in Reciprocity		
What It Is	**Why It Matters**	**What It Looks/Sounds Like**
Willingly moving oneself from isolation and separateness to a connection to and concern for community. Recognizing the worth and dignity of all those with whom one works. Taking joint responsibility to complete work with others in a mutually respectful manner. Recognizing that working together is essential to creating anything significant and that accomplishing tasks requires engagement and effort beyond one's self.	Honoring individual team members and valuing each person's gifts and contributions to the community is critical for a workplace that is grounded in a shared future. Is essential to creating and moving forward significant initiatives in a workplace. Enables organizations to build and achieve their collective potential.	Demonstrating a belief in the worth and dignity of all individuals with whom one works by modeling supportive and productive team behaviors: active listening, questioning, offering suggestions, and verbal and nonverbal behaviors that exhibit respect, show personal regard. Using language choices that demonstrate a belief in each group member's contributions. Willingly participating in experiences that support the group's mandate and vision. Consistently supporting others and their development as group members.

Engage in Reciprocity: Key Concepts

Research states what many of us know intuitively: how we work together matters. Researchers are clear that a collective working together is more effective than any individual (Donohoo, 2017; Hattie 2016). Tony Bryk and Barbara Schneider (2002) assert that relational trust between the adults in schools correlates to higher student achievement. Demonstration of trustworthy behaviors is essential. Amy Edmondson at Harvard (2012) researched the importance of psychological safety in order to work better as a collective. Adult-to-adult communication in schools matters. As educators in a human-centered field, we live out loud our elemental beliefs in the worth and dignity of all human beings (our students, their families, the community, colleagues, and the world). It is foundational to our work. As an individual team member, your ability to collaborate, your willingness to engage thoughtfully and respectfully with the collective, and your capacity to engage in reciprocity are critical to the work you do in schools. These skills matter for teaching, the health of the school, and the collective well-being of all who are taught and work in a school. As Alan Briskin et al., the authors of *The Power of Collective Wisdom: And the Trap of Collective Folly,* state in their book, this stance of engagement with the collective "can be learned and practiced, becoming a new way of being in relationship with others, a new type of human association leading to unleashing the spirit of cooperation and unlimited co-creation in groups." Consider the dimensions of what it takes to engage in reciprocity.

"Reciprocity (noun): behavior in which two people or groups of people give each other help and advantages; a situation in which two groups agree to help each other by behaving in the same way or by giving each other similar advantages."
—Cambridge Dictionary

Engage in Reciprocity: Dimensions

SEE THE GROUP AS A VALUE-ADD

Seeing the group as a value-add to your work means that you understand how the group adds to your knowledge and development. It means that the group's collective wisdom and its input into your work helps you grow more than you could have done on your own. There are diverse stories and experiences that others share that will help you improve student learning. When you see the group as a value-add in your life and work, you learn from and with your colleagues on multiple levels. In the end, you are better for being a part of the team.

DO INNER WORK TO CONTRIBUTE TO THE WHOLE

Being an effective group member means not only doing your specific tasks or taking care of your work responsibilities, but also means supporting others in their work and development. This requires you to be mindful of cultivating your ability to be an effective group member in terms of being aware of body language and non-verbals, active listening, paraphrasing, asking questions, offering suggestions, praising, apologizing, and allowing for equity. These skills were emphasized in Chapter 3 and Facet #3 and are reiterated here in the context of developing an ability to engage in reciprocity at even higher levels and behaving in mutually respectful ways that honor the worth and dignity of all.

This requires inner work to better contribute to the whole. Your inner work is growing your ability to manage your emotions and energy and your commitment to the team, and your outer work is demonstrating that conviction through body language and respectful words. Inner self-monitoring and self-management as well as self-modification will allow you to better contribute to the group, to become both more influential and more supportive, and help you participate in building a healthier team culture.

WORK WITH COGNITIVE CONFLICT

For a team to go from "good" to "great," the group must push and prod itself and help each team member view issues with more complexity and empathy. As Timothy J. Clark states in *The 4 Stages of Psychological Safety: Defining the Path to Inclusion and Innovation* (2020), a team needs to work with more *intellectual friction* and less *social friction*. Decreasing social friction supports the group to feel safe, take risks, and share vulnerabilities. Increasing intellectual friction and creative abrasion supports the group to engage in discussions focused on ideas and not individuals. Less social friction and more intellectual friction allows team members to stretch their thinking, hear new perspectives, challenge themselves, and innovate as a group. When team members engage in this type of encouraging and supportive conversation, the group has the potential to move into new territory.

In order to achieve this type of dialogue, individuals must build their own skills to engage in cognitive and substantive discourse in order to see bias, hear from new voices, and honor new ways of doing and seeing things. In *Unlocking Group Potential to Improve Schools* (2012), Robert J. Garmston and Valerie von Frank discuss the difference between cognitive conflict and affective conflict. "Cognitive conflict involves disagreements about substantive differences of opinion," the authors write. "It improves team effectiveness and produces better decisions, increased commitment, increased cohesiveness, increased empathy, and increased understanding." Affective conflict, on the other hand, "focuses on personalized anger or resentment, usually directed at specific individuals rather than ideas." Affective conflict "often emerges when C-type conflict becomes corrupted because members lack the skills or norms to disagree gracefully." Building your group's ability to discuss issues rather than individuals is key to substantive discourse and building psychological trust. It is a curriculum that can be studied and learned.

UNDERSTAND "WE INFLUENCE I" AND "I INFLUENCES WE"

The old adage often repeated in schools is that there is no "I" in team. That's a myth. Individuals matter. When recognized and valued, individual points of views and diverse ways of seeing the world contribute greatly to the fabric of the collective and the shared future of a school. And the group as a collective also needs to be seen as a value-add to each team member's work. It is a reciprocal partnership. The collective needs to hear many perspectives and value each teammate's stories and gifts. Listening with open minds and hearts to multiple, varied, and valuable perspectives creates the influence of each "I" on the "We," and the "We" can therefore be influenced by each "I." We all are shaped unconsciously or consciously by the environment in which we live and work, and we shape and are shaped by those who surround us.

As we discover through crises and day-to-day engagement with others, we all are interconnected and interdependent. As Stewart Levine wrote in *The Book of Agreement: 10 Essential Elements for Getting the Results You Want* (2002):

> Because all of us are smarter than any one of us, we have come to recognize that the only way we can stay successful is to learn from and teach each other. We believe that is the key to long-term success as an organization. Vicariously, each individual will have the knowledge that he/she was a contribution to a collaborative team of learners... Our bottom line goal is to get people to think beyond their own territoriality, to share, and to respect what others have to contribute. We believe the potential personal and professional rewards will more than compensate for the time we invest in embracing a new cultural mantra.

HONOR OTHERS' DIGNITY

Mutual respect is something we live out loud. Engaging in reciprocity means we show others that we believe in their worth as human beings and we honor one another and what we each bring to the table. In her book *Dignity: The Essential Role It Plays in Resolving Conflict* (2013), Donna Hicks writes about ten key elements of dignity, including the need to recognize and honor all identities, everyone's talents, and each person's hard work. We need to create environments in which everyone is acknowledged, feels a sense of belonging, and is treated justly. Your capacity to believe in others' worth can be strengthened through reflection and work with thoughtfulness and care. The development of our ability to engage with the spirit of reciprocity asks nothing less.

"...[A]s adults, we orient differently to collaboration and its inherent opportunities and challenges and need different kinds of supports and stretches to really make the collaborative shift from 'I' to 'we' in our work." —Eleanor Drago-Severson, Teachers College, Columbia University

DIMENSIONS—ENGAGE IN RECIPROCITY

See the Group as a Value-Add

Do the Inner Work To Contribute to the Whole

Work with Cognitive Conflict

Understand "We Influences I" and "I Influences We"

Honor Others' Dignity

Facet #4: Engage in Reciprocity Characteristics & Continuum

Characteristics	Stage 1	Stage 2	Stage 3
Sees self as a group member. Is aware that one person cannot accomplish large goals without community. Understands that work involves learning and cooperating with others.	I am aware of the need for working on a team to achieve the goals of the school. I am learning to articulate how collaborating with others helps improve everyone's work. I am aware of professional responsibilities and obligations. I am not intentionally difficult during team meetings.	I understand it is essential to have a community in order to further the group's goals. I see myself as someone who helps and influences the group toward achieving goals. I can clearly articulate the benefits of working collaboratively and how influence is reciprocal. I am actively learning additional skills to become an effective and productive group member.	I know deeply how the group influences individuals and I am continually mindful of adjusting my behavior to support the team in achieving its vision/goals. I seek out voices not always heard, understanding that all voices are important to achieving significant progress. I understand how to manage strengths and weaknesses in a team to be an effective group member. I modify my behaviors in order to be more effective in the group.
Recognizes that the group is interconnected and that individuals affect and are affected by the whole. Knows cognitive conflict can help a group move forward.	I am aware that use of norms and ways of speaking allow the group to be more productive, but I don't always follow them. I do not always self-manage and self-monitor. I tolerate disagreements. I try to not to add to them. I am not often able to advocate for an idea without seeming preachy or angry.	I live the norms of the group and reflect on how specific actions affect the group's productivity. I use nonverbals and language that respects the group and the dignity of all. I can distinguish between affective and cognitive conflict and between intellectual and social friction. I find disagreement challenging, but I work on better managing myself during challenging interactions.	I know that every team member is responsible to and should help all group members be more productive in how they use language, address conflict, and monitor the team for productivity, and I identify which voices haven't been heard. I am actively working on wording to disagree skillfully. I can self-manage during difficult moments. I use a variety of methods or protocols to manage discussions.
Knows that the individual is influenced by the group and can individually influence the group. Recognizes that everyone has inherent worth and deserves respect.	I can superficially explain how an individual can make a difference to the group and how they affect the group by their contributions or lack thereof. I understand all individuals are of worthy of respect. I am unsure how to live out this understanding of respect for others in one's actions and behaviors.	I am able to articulate in detail what is intentionally said to influence. I try to explain how others have been influential to me. I am working on taking even more specific actions to demonstrate respect for others. I am still challenged in some cases and I don't always give the benefit of the doubt to those who are deemed challenging.	I am sensitive to how power and privilege play out in who is and is not contributing to the group. I can articulate how the group can assist individuals in changing perspectives and expand inclusivity. I am deeply aware and active with demonstrating the belief that all in the group have dignity and worth. I am mindful as to how to demonstrate that belief out loud.

Engage in Reciprocity: Self-Talk by Stages

Another way to look at the characteristics of this facet is to experience what self-talk might look like at each stage. What might you say to yourself or to others at each stage of engaging in reciprocity?

Facet #4: Engage in Reciprocity Self-Talk by Stages			
	Stage 1	Stage 2	Stage 3
What am I saying to myself?	"I hope this meeting is well organized. I don't like meetings in general – I commonly feel like they are a waste of time." "I know being a team player is the right thing to do, but I don't always get a lot from the meetings. Sometimes it feels easier to just work on my own." "I don't always trust my colleagues to be supportive or kind if I share my challenges and dilemmas. I worry they will question my competence and judge me."	"I am looking forward to seeing my teammates because I have a few things I would like to run past them. They make my ideas better." "I am working on 'suggesting versus telling' in groups. I am a group member in progress working being more supportive and less judgmental." "I want to build my confidence to listen even when something might change how I do things."	"I am on board and want to be a supportive and contributing part of my collective. I know this will take work." "I am working intentionally to make it easier for my group to discuss difficult issues and problems." "I know what skills are needed to have productive discussions and be open to feedback. I respect others' input. And I recognize that my journey to develop my communication skills is never-ending. I see my part in the bigger picture." "I work intentionally to contribute to the wellbeing of my group."
What am I saying to others?	"I am not used to giving input to a group. Can you give me examples of what others expect me to say and not say as I would like to do it right." "I find it hard to listen to feedback without being emotional and possibly defensive." "I sometimes find it hard not to add to the noise of a discussion but to contribute positively and move us back on track."	"I like to hear new ideas from the group even if I don't agree, and I like sharing my ideas too." "I am working on making sure my non-verbals and facial expressions are not perceived as disrespectful." "If everyone remembers to keep the discussion respectful, I can handle a little disagreement. I need to work on expressing myself during moments of challenge and I do so respectfully." "I need to offer my input in ways that will benefit the group, and I know I don't always do so." "I struggle with input, but I honestly consider it."	"I'm communicating my own ideas, but I also openly support my teammates' ideas and the group's goals. I'm trying to make sure others feel safe when bringing a divergent opinion to the group." "I seek input to push me and to make sure we are all in the loop." "Conflict is human. I can handle creative friction and help the group keep discussions substantive and intellectually focused." "What could I do or stop doing that would make it easier to work with me?" "I ask for feedback and am happy to offer some. I am working on asking what type of input group members would like to have when I offer feedback."

Engage in Reciprocity: Self-Assessment

Amateurs focus on tearing other people down. Professionals focus on making everyone better... Amateurs think disagreements are threats. Professionals see them as an opportunity to learn.

–Shane Parrish, "The Difference Between Amateurs and Professionals," Farnam Street blog

Another way to look at engaging in reciprocity is by self-assessing behaviors that align with its related characteristics. What might you do or say if you were progressing through the stages of developing awareness around engaging in reciprocity? For each statement, select the response that most represents where you feel you are.

- I am aware that my department and my team influence my thinking, and I can articulate how they influence my work.
  - ☐ I haven't thought about it.
  - ☐ I have given this some thought, and I'm getting better at this.
  - ☐ I have given this a lot of thought, and I am very good at this.
- I influence others on my team and in my workplace.
  - ☐ I haven't thought about it.
  - ☐ I have given this some thought, and I'm getting better at this.
  - ☐ I have given this a lot of thought, and I am very good at this.
- I am aware that I am one part of my workplace, my department, and my team, and I see how I contribute to the bigger vision and goal.
  - ☐ I haven't thought about it.
  - ☐ I have given this some thought, and I'm getting better at this.
  - ☐ I have given this a lot of thought, and I am very good at this.
- I understand that I can achieve larger goals only through group collaboration.
  - ☐ I haven't thought about it.
  - ☐ I have given this some thought, and I'm getting better at this.
  - ☐ I have given this a lot of thought, and I am very good at this.
- I am aware of the importance of having all team members feel their contributions are valued.
  - ☐ I haven't thought about it.
  - ☐ I have given this some thought, and I'm getting better at this.
  - ☐ I have given this a lot of thought, and I am very good at this.
- I know the key skills needed to be an effective group member, and I recognize how those skills help me contribute to the group.
  - ☐ I haven't thought about it.
  - ☐ I have given this some thought, and I'm getting better at this.
  - ☐ I have given this a lot of thought, and I am very good at this.
- I know my strengths and weaknesses as a group member and work to address my weaknesses.
  - ☐ I haven't thought about it.
  - ☐ I have given this some thought, and I'm getting better at this.
  - ☐ I have given this a lot of thought, and I am very good at this.
- I recognize that it is my responsibility to monitor my behavior in a team meeting.
  - ☐ I haven't thought about it.
  - ☐ I have given this some thought, and I'm getting better at this.
  - ☐ I have given this a lot of thought, and I am very good at this.

- I acknowledge my obligation to the team to make sure all voices are involved and are heard.
  - ☐ I haven't thought about it.
  - ☐ I have given this some thought, and I'm getting better at this.
  - ☐ I have given this a lot of thought, and I am very good at this.
- I recognize that cognitive conflict and intellectual friction can help a group move forward.
  - ☐ I haven't thought about it.
  - ☐ I have given this some thought, and I'm getting better at this.
  - ☐ I have given this a lot of thought, and I am very good at this.
- I know how social conflict can harm the psychological safety of a team.
  - ☐ I haven't thought about it.
  - ☐ I have given this some thought, and I'm getting better at this.
  - ☐ I have given this a lot of thought, and I am good at this.
- I understand that group structures, norms, and protocols can support cognitive and psychologically safe discussions, and I willingly participate in those protocols with awareness and skill.
  - ☐ I haven't thought about it.
  - ☐ I have given this some thought, and I'm getting better at this.
  - ☐ I have given this a lot of thought, and I am very good at this.
- I take ownership for helping my team become as productive as it can be.
  - ☐ I haven't thought about it.
  - ☐ I have given this some thought, and I'm getting better at this.
  - ☐ I have given this a lot of thought, and I am very good at this
- I know that my work is influenced by being on a team and what I learn from my teammates.
  - ☐ I haven't thought about it.
  - ☐ I have given this some thought, and I'm getting better at this.
  - ☐ I have given this a lot of thought, and I am very good at this.
- I believe each member of my team has worth and deserves to be treated with dignity in our meetings.
  - ☐ I haven't thought about it.
  - ☐ I have given this some thought, and I am getting better at this.
  - ☐ I have given this a lot of thought, and I am very good at this.

Now that you have selected your responses:

Look. Look for patterns. Where are you most aware/least aware?

Reflect. Which statements surprise you and merit future thought and attention?

Consider. How might learning more about yourself in response to these statements support your development and assist you in your work?

Engage in Reciprocity: Exercises for Development

All of these exercises align with the parts of the continuum and the self-assessment in one way or another. There is no specific sequence for these exercises. All thinking and reflection is good.

Remember:

- These are intentionally called exercises, in contrast to activities. The goal is to develop in this facet. This type of growth doesn't always feel good or easy.
- You can decide which exercises align with your specific focus within the continuum for this facet. You can do some of the exercises—or you can do them all. Self-determination rules.
- There is no expectation that the exercises be done perfectly; there is no perfect score.
- There is no time limit on how long an exercise should take.

EXERCISE 1: Bottom Line Professionalism in a Team

Purpose: To have a baseline understanding of what professionalism can look like in a school environment.

Guiding Tips: This isn't an exhaustive description of the skills to be a professional. It is a basic list, encompassing foundational behaviors that are expected from all team members, and a starting point from which to assess one's collaborative skills.

Directions: Consider these questions and determine your answers. Take note of where you are challenged by specific behaviors.

- Am I mentally present in meetings? Do I show up on time or late? Am I present emotionally and mentally at staff meetings? Department meetings? At team meetings?

  ____

  ____

- Do I know, understand, respect, and follow my job description? My department's goals and objectives? The mission and vision of my organization?

  ____

  ____

- If I'm asked to complete paperwork, attend a meeting on behalf of the department, or do work for the team, do I get it done? On time?

  ____

  ____

- Do I share enthusiasm for the work? If so, how do I demonstrate that to my teammates?

  ____

  ____

- Do I outwardly demonstrate that I enjoy my work? Enjoy my workplace? Enjoy my colleagues? How do I show my teammates that I am engaged?

  ____

  ____

- Are my communications with others done in a timely manner?

  ____

  ____

- Do I hold myself to a high standard for what I do and produce? If so, how do I demonstrate that?

  ____

  ____

- Do I continually refine my skill set? If so, how?

  ____

  ____

- Am I aware of my workplace's values, norms, and the way the organization sees itself? Do I work well with these values? If so, how? Do I embody these values and norms?

  ____

  ____

- Do I hone my communication skills in addition to working on my technical expertise? If so, how?

  ____

  ____

- Do I show consideration for others' feelings? Do I say things like, "Hello," "Thank you," "I'm sorry," and "What can I do to help?"

  ____

  ____

- Do I gossip? Do I say negative things about colleagues to others?

  ____

  ____

- Am I aware of my assumptions and values, and do I know when my assumptions get in the way of the team's progress toward goals?

  ____

  ____

- Am I able to stand outside myself and see how I might affect others or be seen by others?

  ____

  ____

- If I am given feedback, do I listen to it and react appropriately, changing my behavior if necessary?

____

____

- Can I recognize and understand that someone else's decision making might be more rational or emotional than mine, and can I work with that person?

____

____

- Am I open to changing my approach to completing a task rather than taking a "my way or the highway" view?

____

____

- Am I willing to hear perspectives different from my own? Do I honor other perspectives by listening to understand, or do I shut down when I hear them?

____

____

- Do I cooperate with other departments in my workplace so we better reach those we serve? Do I fill out any needed paperwork or reports and do so with a positive attitude?

____

____

- Am I able to listen with understanding and empathy?

____

____

- Do I use language that demonstrates my belief that my teammates are competent and capable? Do I offer suggestions (Perhaps you could...) rather than statements (You should...) so people can take action on their own behalf?

____

____

- Am I aware when I am not allowing equitable participation in a meeting by talking too much and dominating or too little and not contributing?

____

____

Post-Exercise Reflection:

- What did I notice about myself in my responses?
- What might steps might I take next to work on any of these foundational skills?

EXERCISE 2: Creating Positive Affective States

Purpose: To recognize the impact an individual has on a team's emotional state and other members' safety.

Guiding Tips: This list is not exhaustive and is not "the top 5 behaviors that make or break a group's efficacy." Yet these behaviors affect a group, and teammates are responsible for managing themselves during group interactions. Every team member intentionally or unintentionally contributes to a feeling of psychological safety through verbal and nonverbal language as well through actions.

Directions: Respond to the questions and ask yourself where your strengths are and where you have learning edges.

- Do I manage my anxiety appropriately? Do I yell at colleagues? Do I sigh deeply in response to others? Do I turn my back to group members?

  ____

  ____

- Am I aware of my body language when I am with others? Do I have appropriate, respectful, and proper sense of decorum in specific settings?

  ____

  ____

- Do I have a sense of my own and others' personal space in a given setting?

  ____

  ____

- When communicating with others, do I ask for perspectives and seek out others' opinions?

  ____

  ____

- Do I demonstrate my ability to listen and pause? Do I demonstrate that I understand what I hear?

  ____

  ____

- Do I manage impulsivity or do I interrupt others? Do I insert my point of view more often than others do?

  ____

  ____

- Do I enter the group with a sense of humor? Can I laugh at myself?

  ____

  ____

Psychological safety is when you have a culture in which it isn't expensive to be yourself.

–Timothy R. Clark, author, *The Four Stages of Psychological Safety*

CREATING PSYCHOLOGICAL SAFETY

"Psychological safety represents the extent to which the team views the social climate as conducive to interpersonal risk."

—Amy Edmondson, Harvard Business School professor

Post-Exercise Reflection:

- What most interested me in responding to this assessment?
- How might I use these questions before I begin a meeting? How could the questions benefit myself and others after a meeting?

EXERCISE 3: Be an Upstander

Purpose: To learn ways to speak up rather than tune out when we hear others make negative, generalized statements that create psychologically and emotionally unsafe spaces. We are responsible for speaking up to address uncomfortable, untrue, generalizing, or racist, sexist, homophobic comments.

Guiding Tips: Check your workplace handbook or human resources to determine whether your organization has clear expectations about how and when employees should speak up. There might be specific school or district norms.

Directions:

Part 1: Look at these case studies and consider how, as an upstander, you would take responsibility for responding. What might you say? What could you say?

- Scenario #1: You're passing a classroom and you hear one person "blow up" at another. Person one yells at person two and even uses curse words. What might you say to this colleague to show that you heard what they said and that such language is not acceptable?

____

____

____

- Scenario #2: During a team meeting, a colleague offers an idea and another rolls their eyes and says, "That's a stupid idea that's not going to work." What could you say in that moment?

____

____

____

- Scenario #3: The group starts a discussion and someone makes negative comments about the students the school serves. What do you say?

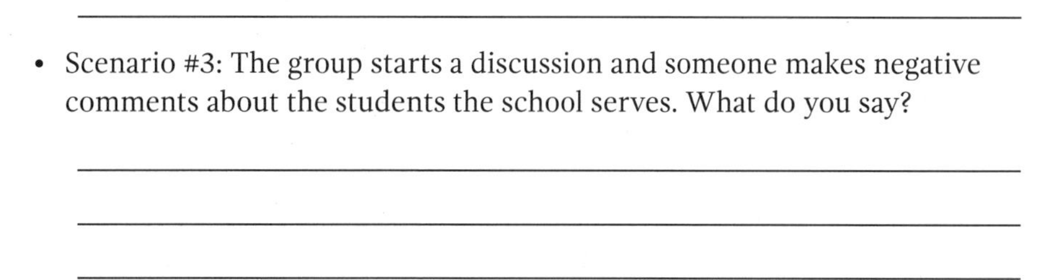

____

____

____

Part 2: Review possible "seize the moment" responses. Which could you use in the scenarios given above? Which do you think you'd feel comfortable using? How do you see your responsibility to respond?

- "I'm not willing to agree with that generalization."
- "Some of the words you just used make me uncomfortable."

VERBAL PAPER CUTS/ LUCKY THEM

In this video Jennifer describes how aware we need to be with our language with others and how it can harm or heal.

https://bit.ly/3tU5vmb

- “I don’t agree with what you just said. Could you please share more about what you mean?”
- “That comment makes me feel uncomfortable.”
- “That seems unfair to me.”
- “I have a different opinion.”
- “We value everyone here.”
- “Ouch.”
- “That stings.”

Post-Exercise Reflection:

- What thoughts come up when I read the scenarios and imagine using the responses?
- How do I think these responses demonstrate mutual respect for all? Does reading and thinking about these possible responses make being an upstander seem more achievable?
- What responses have I used in the past when someone has said something professionally unsound, psychologically unsafe, or emotionally damaging? What new responses might I add to my repertoire?

EXERCISE 4: Living Lambert Out Loud

Purpose: To learn three key ideas about adult learning that align with engaging in reciprocity.

Guiding Tips: Some find it tricky to move from a theoretical understanding of the concepts in this exercise to describing practical next steps. Translating these ideas into action means moving from the vague to the specific. For example, saying to yourself, “Oh, I need to be kinder” is too vague. Move toward specific behaviors and actions. For example, you could write down, “Make eye contact and smile during a teammate’s share.” Specificity is the key to action in this exercise.

Directions: Read about adult learning assumptions which draw from ideas in Dr. Linda Lambert’s book *Building Leadership Capacity in Schools* (2002). Lambert proposes three concepts to keep in mind as you work in your team. Consider how these concepts relate to your work and how your actions and language can demonstrate your understanding so you work more productively and supportively in your team.

Assumption #1: Adults have a drive toward competence. This is directly linked to self-image and efficacy. We all want to feel competent and in control. Working in a team can feel both exciting and threatening. And with a desire to look competent while learning new ideas, internal tensions can develop. Team members may ask themselves, “What if I look dumb? What if I say something and someone rolls their eyes? What if I have a question? What if I make a mistake?” This concern about feeling capable and being seen as competent is human and normal. Using positive presuppositions in communication, especially around new information, lets team members know that we believe they are capable.

Use language that acknowledges and highlights expertise and capacity and indicates that you see strengths and acknowledge ownership and decisions. Try phrases such as these:

- We've moved into new territory before, so what do you suggest with...
- I'm interested in hearing your thoughts about how we could move ahead.
- I know you have had success with similar changes. What should we remember and keep in mind about...

Assumption #2: Learning is both an opportunity and a risk; it requires an ability to sit with discomfort and change. In *Mindset: The New Psychology of Success* (2006), Carol Dweck writes that we need to encourage a growth mindset in students, and explains that adults, too, need to think this way. A growth mindset is developing abilities through dedication and hard work. Leaders encourage growth mindsets by repeatedly acknowledging out loud that new projects are risky, and that the team might not get it right the first time, but through perseverance can achieve success. Learning requires risk, vulnerability in front of others, and might not be successful immediately—and that's okay. Learning comes when something doesn't work right the first time, and the problem is addressed again. Discomfort isn't all bad— and we need to say that over and over. If we use a growth mindset, we find that challenge and continuous learning are part of progress. When we expect work to be iterative, we are better able to move forward with less discomfort in our psyches and in our communities.

Assumption #3: Learning is the continual process of identity formation. At times, we are less than generous with those with whom we work. We become judgmental about their learning speed and so much more. We want our adult work teammates to be comfortable with change, mature in their responses to uncertainty, and quick to respond successfully. Considering the demands we all face in dealing with innovations and rapid changes in the world, unrealistic expectations are unfair and unreasonable. (And we often don't live up to our ideals either!) Everyone is in the process of identity formation and growing into who they can become.

Post-Exercise Reflection:

- As I develop as a more effective and supportive teammate, how might living these three adult learning assumptions out loud help me and help our team?
- How do these three adult-learning assumptions connect to building my abilities as a learning community member?
- What can I do or say related to each assumption to live these ideas "out loud?"

EXERCISE 5: Norms for Collaborative Work

(Source: Annotated Norms, Norms for Collaboration, www.thinkingcollaborative.com)

Purpose: To assess your ability to use seven specific skills in collaborative work.

Guiding Tips: This set of norms, or skills, is from the Thinking Collaborative. These skills need to be *overtly* taught, consciously worked on, and strategically reflected upon to become the natural way for a team to work together. This preview/review exercise is not an end in itself but a beginning of both an individual's and a team's growth, depending on how it is done.

Directions: Assess yourself on each collaborative norm. Do you do them well, somewhat well, or not very well?

1. **Pausing.** Pausing after asking a question allows time for people to think.
2. **Paraphrasing.** Using paraphrases shows you are listening and working to understand group members. Choose phrasing that is comfortable for you. For example, "So" or "As you are" or "You're thinking" as you start your paraphrases.
3. **Posing Questions.** Ask questions that allow teammates to explore perceptions, assumptions, and interpretations. Use an inviting manner. For example, "What ideas are you exploring given what you know now?" Support each other to increase everyone's clarity and precision of thinking. Inquire about others' ideas before advocating for your own.
4. **Putting Ideas on the Table.** Label your comments. For example: "Here is one idea..." or "One thought I have is..." or "Here is a possible approach..." or "Another consideration might be..."
5. **Providing Data.** Offer data, both qualitative and quantitative, in a variety of forms to support team members in constructing shared understanding from the work.
6. **Paying Attention to Self and Others.** Be conscious of yourself and others. Stay aware of what you say and how it is said, as well as how others respond. Pay attention to learning styles when you participate in group meetings and conversations.
7. **Presuming Positive Intention.** Start by assuming that others' intentions are positive in order to promote meaningful dialogue and discussion. Work to use unintentional put-downs.

Post-Exercise Reflection:

- Which of these collaborative norms is a strength of mine?
- Which of these collaborative norms is a stretch and learning edge for me?
- What steps could I take next to work on a specific norm?
- How might my team assess ourselves and take action to build these skills?

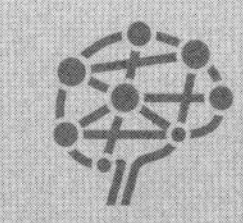

Find more information about the seven norms at Thinking Collaborative. https://bit.ly/3vWhcuB

And for more information on how collaborative norms might look in action, visit: https://bit.ly/31iHVU2

EXERCISE 6: Rationales for Using Protocols

Purpose: To provide adults some rationale for using protocols to talk effectively about their problems of practice. This exercise helps increase awareness around the purpose and usefulness of protocols.

Guiding Tips: Team members sometimes feel that protocols provide too much structure. They can find it patronizing to be hemmed in by so many constraints on how to talk, for how long, and when to share. However, protocols allow for professional and productive conversations to occur smoothly within a given time limit, provide a structure to do so effectively, honor equity of voice, and afford opportunity for all to share a point of view. It could help to mention that using a protocol constitutes a "renting" of the protocol for the proposed time rather than "buying" it and always needing to use it. At the end of a meeting, ask if others agree that the protocol helped create a culture of equity, assured all voices were heard, and assisted in an increase in risk-taking and productivity. If the protocol did *not* help maintain psychological safety and promote professional conversations, the team can consider the continued use of protocols or provide other suggestions for more efficacy.

Directions: Give voice to why protocols are useful for teams working actively on Facet #4 (engaging in reciprocity), and use a shared multiple perspectives protocol in order to have the discussion. (Adapted from the 'Final Word Protocol' from National School Reform Faculty.) Follow the specific directions below.

- Read all the quotations below regarding the purpose and intent of the use of protocols. Determine which quote (or two) makes most sense to you and/or in what way you see it expresses the positive usage of protocols.
- One person directs the group and shares a quote. Team members do not interrupt the individual or share their feelings. No cross talk occurs. One person shares their quote, does not explain why they chose it, but just reads it out loud.
- The next person now responds to the first person's quote and shares their opinions on the idea/quote. No one interrupts or piggybacks on this person's response.
- Responses to the quote are offered by all until all group members have had an opportunity to share their reactions to the initial quote.
- After everyone in the group has shared, the person who introduced the quote at the start now takes time to share to the group why they chose the quote. They also share how the others' contributions changed or affected their viewpoint of the ideas in the quote.
- Continue until all members of the group have had their turn to share a quote.

THE VALUE OF PROTOCOLS

(quotations selected from *The Power of Protocols: An Educator's Guide to Better Practice* by Joseph P. McDonald, Nancy Mohr, Alan Dichter, and Elizabeth C. McDonald.)

"The contradiction at the heart of protocol is that it has to standardize in order to liberate."

"[Protocols] are inherently participative. And they not only require—or we would say foster—a substantial degree of democratization, they also insist on a certain quality of democratization—one that prizes diversity, universal participation, and a wide cultivation of what we call facilitative leadership."

"We professionals should take charge of our own learning. It is important to note the plural in the phrase *educating ourselves.* No [person] works alone, although we seem to. Yes, we make lots of private moves, and our work demands an individual capacity for spontaneity, improvisation, and good judgment. But all our efforts, for better or worse, are mediated by the efforts of our colleagues. What they do matters as much to the learning of our students and the running of our programs as what we do. Thus our colleagues' values, standards and methods are our business—as ours are their business—and the problems of practice are inescapably mutual ones."

"One good way for us to educate ourselves is to pause periodically in our practice and become deliberate students of our [work]... It is where the strengths and weaknesses of our practices—individual and collective—become most apparent."

"Peter Elbow argues that the [individual] must learn to temper what he calls methodological belief with methodological doubt—systematically subjecting ideas, plans, and output to both impulses, giving each its due. Protocols force transparency by segmenting elements of a conversation whose boundaries otherwise blur."

"Professional learning communities are where [individuals] can learn and unlearn whatever scrutiny, responsiveness, and strategic flexibility require. This is where they can educate themselves accordingly. Such education... can fully meet the needs of professionals really attentive to their [work] and their own contexts."

Post-Exercise Reflection:

- How did both the content of the quotations and the protocol used for processing the quotations enhance my understanding of the benefits of using protocols?
- What continues to challenge me about the use of protocols?

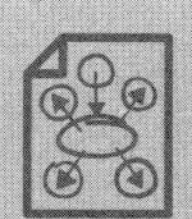

ORGANIZATIONS AND BOOKS WITH INFORMATION ABOUT PROTOCOLS

The National School Reform Faculty (NSRF), www.nsrfharmony.org

The Power of Protocols: An Educator's Guide to Better Practice, by Joseph P. McDonald, Nancy Mohr, Alan Dichter, and Elizabeth C. McDonald (Teachers College Press, April 2003).

School Reform Initiative https://bit.ly/2PwPOhO

EXERCISE 7: Do You Want to Be Heard? Be More Socially Persuasive

Purpose: To consider how effectively we communicate our point of view to others in our group. To build capacity to influence others.

Guiding Tips: If you find yourself thinking, "How do I get my ideas across to my colleagues?" this could be a useful set of questions to consider. This is a review of capacities and skills that will build your influence with others.

Directions: Take a look at the questions below. What actions do you do successfully? Which ones are more challenging? Is your skill level situational? In what ways?

- Do I listen to and understand the needs and challenges facing those who I want to influence?
- Do people come to me when they need help solving problems?
- Do people I work with characterize me as a warm and good listener?
- Do I show respect for others' feelings by listening non-judgmentally?
- Do I demonstrate strong commitment to issues that will make my teammates successful and act in the team's best interest rather than my own?
- Do I seem like and behave as though I can change my mind?
- Do I explain risks and rewards when I present my ideas to others?
- Do people know me as someone who knows my own limits and shows humility?
- Am I known as a person who is polite and open to those who disagree with me?

Post-Exercise Reflection:

- What do I notice?
- What are my strengths?
- Where are my learning edges?
- What next step is within my sphere of control that I can take to build this skill set?

Responses to Those Who Challenge the Reason We Need to Work in Groups

WHAT IF SOMEONE SAYS...?

"I'm an introvert, and I don't like working in groups?"

A possible response could be, "It is important that all voices are in the room, and we encourage and expect everyone to participate. And we need your ideas. We value everyone's contribution style. If you need more time to think in silence, please ask. We also are committed to not wasting time or causing group members distress. If you feel that we have gone over time, please let the group know."

"I prefer working alone, and that working in groups is inefficient and ineffective?"

A possible response could be, "I have been in unproductive meetings, too. We are committed to not wasting time. If we are off task, let us know in a supportive way. If we go over time, share that with the group. We believe the value of working together is that all our skills and a diversity of ideas will lead to better outcomes for students. If you feel the group is not being as productive as it can be, please share some ideas for improving the process."

EXERCISE 8: Having Hard Conversations—Quick Scripts

Purpose: To provide practice for in-the-moment responses when you see something that is professionally unsound, physically unsafe, or emotionally damaging that is occurring in a meeting or elsewhere.

Guiding Tips: Try to formulate and express your response between one and forty-eight hours after something occurs that needs feedback. After that time, your response is less powerful and productive.

Directions: Intentionally working to create an environment that honors diverse stories often asks us to speak up when others don't live up to the commitment to a safe and respectful workplace for all. When you notice that an action or comment is hurtful or inappropriate, share your perspective using the following sentence stems.

1. "I noticed you (said or did)..."
2. "I felt or thought... "
3. "You might consider saying/doing/not doing/not saying...in future."

Example 1: "I noticed that you said, 'What do you want?' pretty gruffly when our colleague came to see you. If I were them, I might feel intimidated about coming to talk to you. Did you sense that they were a bit taken aback?"

Example 2: "When you did (behavior), I thought/felt (reaction). It would be helpful to me if you could do (behavior) instead. Can you see this from my perspective? Thanks for letting me share that."

Example 3: "When you come to our meeting later than our agreed time, I feel that the meeting isn't important to you. It would be helpful for the team that if you are going to be late that you let us know. Is that a possibility?"

Post-Exercise Reflection:

- Could I follow these quick scripts?
- What would I change so that I can?

EXERCISE 9: Quote Journaling

Purpose: To see how others have written about the concept of interdependence.

Guiding Tips: There is no perfect quote. Pick the one that most immediately connects to you or most challenges you at this time.

Directions: Take five to ten minutes to write your response to the quote. What are your a-has (insights), hmms (ponderings), ouches (awareness of weakness)?

Quotes

- "Maturity comes in three stages: dependence, independence and interdependence."—Jenna Jameson, American actress
- "The fundamental law of human beings is interdependence. A person is a person through other persons."—Archbishop Desmond Tutu, South African Nobel Peace Prize winner

- "Interdependence is a choice only independent people can make." —Stephen Covey, American author
- "We men and women are all in the same boat, in a stormy sea. We owe to each other a terrible and tragic loyalty."—Gilbert K. Chesterton, English writer and philosopher
- "Interdependence is and ought to be as much the ideal of man as self-sufficiency. Man is a social being. Without interrelation with society he cannot realize his oneness with the universe or suppress his egotism. His social interdependence enables him to test his faith and to prove himself on the touchstone of reality."—Mahatma Gandhi, Indian anti-colonial nationalist
- "Interdependence is a higher value than independence."—Stephen Covey, American author
- "Never doubt that a small group of thoughtful, committed citizens can change the world; indeed, it's the only thing that ever has."—attributed to Margaret Mead, American cultural anthropologist
- "No man is an island entire of itself; every man is a piece of the continent." —John Donne, English poet
- "I can never be what I ought to be until you are what you ought to be." —Martin Luther King Jr., social activist
- "According to [Clinton's] explanation, ubuntu means 'I am, because you are.' In fact, the word ubuntu is just part of the Zulu phrase 'Umuntu ngumuntu ngabantu,' which literally means that a person is a person through other people."—Nkem Ifejika, British journalist
- "There is one word that can be the guide for your life. It is the word reciprocity." – Pearl S. Buck, American writer
- "Social peace requires reciprocity."—Ralph Peters, retired US Army lieutenant colonel and author
- "Humans and the creaturely world have as their vocation the duty to support and complete one another, not to compete against and destroy one another."—Michael Perry, American author
- "We never know how our small activities will affect others through the invisible fabric of connectedness."—Grace Lee Boggs, American author
- "No matter what accomplishments you make, somebody helped you." —Althea Gibson, American tennis player

____

____

____

____

____

____

FLIGHT FROM LA- WHAT DOES IT TAKE?

In this video, Jennifer considers all the individuals who make a flight from LA to SFO happen and the need for everyone's participation.

https://bit.ly/3d8RFFP

Post-Exercise Reflection:

- What did I notice in my response?
- What did I learn about myself? If I did this exercise with others, which quotes did they choose?
- How might I live out what I learned from this exercise in my interactions today?

EXERCISE 10: Inclusion and Exclusion - Designing Wordles

Purpose: To understand more about how conditions of inclusion (versus conditions of exclusion) allow for productively engaging in reciprocity.

Guiding Tips: Consider these questions as a start of a conversation about creating conditions of equity, inclusion, and belonging. This exercise highlights where engaging with reciprocity interconnects with the facets of suspending certainty and knowing your identity. You can do this exercise with a partner, or better yet, with your team.

Directions:

- Take time for each person on the team (or in trios if need be) to share a story about a group in which they felt included. What factors were present to make it feel like they belonged in the group?
- When everyone is done sharing their story, do a public recording, on a large paper or screen for all to see, of all of the enabling conditions for feeling included.
- Continuing on, take time for each person on the team to share a story of a group in which they felt excluded. What factors were present to make it feel like they were not welcomed in the group?
- When everyone is done sharing, do a public recording, on a large paper or screen for all to see, of all the enabling conditions that contributed to the feelings of exclusion.
- Now as a team, look at the conditions on both papers:
  - What do you notice?
  - How might this exercise support your team in creating meeting norms, environments, or communication practices so everyone feels included and welcomed?

Post-Exercise Reflection:

- What did you learn about yourself that is helpful to know for your future interaction on teams?
- What do you see that could assist you in the goal of increasing the feeling belonging among colleagues on your team? How so?
- How might this exercise and exploration support your work and communications going forward?

Chapter Reflection Questions: Engage in Reciprocity

- In what instances have I been reluctant to explore the ideas addressed here?
- What might I need to unlearn?
- What will it look like to see development and embodiment of an increased understanding of this facet?
- How do I demonstrate that I am a respectful teammate through body language and words? When do I not?
- How do I work with my teammates to face challenges? Do I focus on individuals or ideas in my discourse?
- In what ways can I identify how we are all interconnected and interdependent?
- When do I feel territorial, and in what situations do I find it easiest to contribute to the group?
- How do I show my belief in the worth of every member of my team expressed in our meetings? How do I see that the dignity of all members is recognized? How do I not see it?

ENGAGING WITH RECIPROCITY

(adapted from "I Actually Don't Know How to Be in Community with Others" by Garrett Bucks)

- With whom do I have the opportunity to be in relationship with today? To what extent do I treat those opportunities as gifts rather than obligations?
- How much of my own mental time do I spend thinking about myself—about how I'm perceived, my professional trajectory, and/or my own experiences of disconnection or guilt?
- What happens when I notice those moments? Instead of shaming myself for them, do I recognize them as opportunities to discover how much I crave connection with other people?
- How frequently, after noticing those moments, do I take them as invitations to connect with others, strengthen new bonds, and repair old ones?
- As I spend more of my day connecting with others, what do I learn?

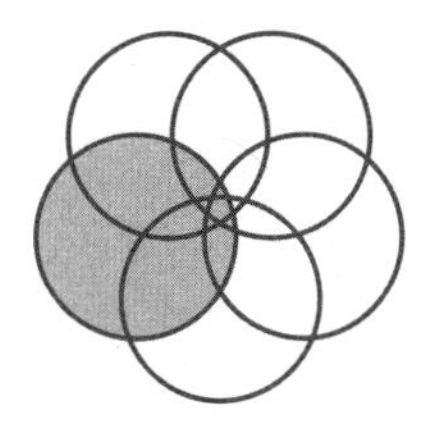

CHAPTER FIVE
Facet #5 - Build Resiliency

Ring the bells that still can ring
Forget your perfect offering
There is a crack, a crack in everything
That's how the light gets in
That's how the light gets in.
—from "Anthem," by Leonard Cohen, singer-songwriter

CHAPTER TAKEAWAYS

As you read, consider these as final reflective questions and make notes as your takeaways.

- Which ideas in this chapter resonate the most with me?
- What has been worthy of my time?
- Which concepts from this chapter have been the most meaningful and stand out for me?

Guiding Questions

- How do I cope with unexpected chaos and high-anxiety situations?
- Can I soothe myself when I am dismissed, diminished, challenged, or ignored?
- In moments of discomfort, can I continue to let in information? Can I make informed, nonreactive choices and keep myself centered?
- Can I identify my purpose and do I use it to ground and center myself in my work?
- Do I have strategies that help me remain centered in my life and at work?

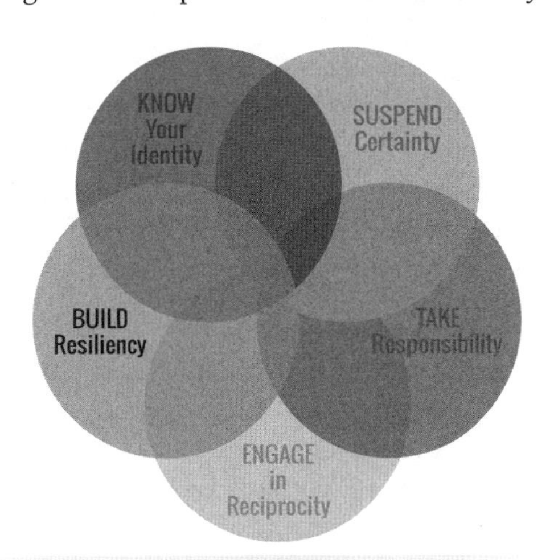

Definition: Building Resiliency

The capacity to recover from or adjust to change with relative ease.

Facet #5: Build Resiliency		
What It Is	**Why It Matters**	**What It Looks/Sounds Like**
The strength and ability to respond to stressful situations, change, disappointment, and loss.	Improves your ability to accept and manage uncomfortable emotions. Helps your ability to influence the work environment in a more positive way. Essential to sustaining a productive, compassionate work environment for all. Sustains you in deeper and strenuous work.	Having time, space, ability, and opportunity to acknowledge difficulties, loss, and disappointment with yourself and others. Recognizing that self-care is inextricably related to team care. Acknowledging that your sphere of control may not be large, but your sphere of influence is greater than you imagine.

Build Resiliency: Key Concepts

Resiliency is the core of contentment in a long life. Developing resiliency does not mean being tough, powering through, or ignoring pain. It is instead the ability to sit with and work through challenges and to adapt and change to the vicissitudes life inevitably brings our way. TED talks and self-help books abound about building resiliency. With ever-changing concerns, competing commitments, and transitions asked of us in our workplace, the need to grow our ability to bounce back is essential to survival and thriving in our personal and professional lives. When children are small, we sometimes allow them to fall without swooping in, so when they get up, they see they are capable of recovering. In our adult lives, we also “fall down.” Life is full of falling—and full of recovery. How do we recover more quickly and with more ease? How do we build our resiliency? Working on a number of dimensions can improve our resiliency.

Build Resiliency: Dimensions

DO SIT-UPS FOR YOUR PSYCHE

Have you entered a roomful of people and felt a weird feeling in the air or sat through a meeting thick with tension? Your and team members’ energy can positively or negatively impact the group. Bioenergetics research demonstrates that one form of algae can absorb energy from other plants (Kruse, 2012). Much like that, people’s energy can ooze out intentionally or unintentionally and affect others. Do you generally radiate negativity or positivity?

For your own and your organization’s or community’s health, it’s important to learn to manage your energy and recover quickly. You can build resolve, strength, and stamina to manage the energy and volatility that comes with your work. You may find solutions in meditation, coursework on anger management, physical exercise, healthy eating, therapeutic support, or other assistance. When you manage your anxiety, you release grief and disappointment in appropriate ways.

ASSESS YOUR FRAGILITY

We all have our learning edges. In this facet, you assess where you don't shore up yourself up proactively. Perhaps you are too prickly when faced with criticism, too vulnerable to moodiness, too indebted, or too under-resourced in important areas of your life. Plan to bolster where you are weak. It will serve you well, and others too.

SEE EVERYTHING AS A GROWTH OPPORTUNITY

It may sound Pollyanna-ish or unrealistic to ask you to experience negative moments as opportunities for growth. If you are homeless, received a diagnosis, or find a foundation of your life has cracked, it most likely isn't the right moment to view the situation as a growth opportunity. When a project hasn't gone well or the feedback you received was less than stellar, and the world isn't collapsing and no one is hurt, you might look at disappointment through a growth lens. How might this experience serve me? What can I learn from this situation? Thinking of it simply as "turning a frown upside down" diminishes the courage it takes to change your emotional state. It can be emotional and psychological heavy lifting to shift a mindset, and it can take tremendous energy. We are all stumbling forward. Yet building resiliency comes from deep breaths, not prolonging pain, and by taking the next step forward.

9/10THS STORY

In this video Jennifer recalls a moment of support she received from a friend that built her resiliency moving forward.

https://bit.ly/3rraQzQ

DON'T EXPECT APPLAUSE

Margaret J. Wheatley, founder of the group, Warriors for the Human Spirit, has a saying for those who get frustrated and disappointed when they aren't acknowledged and their good work appears to be unappreciated: "Don't expect applause." Don't work for kudos or accolades. Do the work you are meant to and you feel is the right work for the team and the organization, and move forward. A lot of hurt feelings arise when we expect others will see us and reward our good work. Your contributions will often go unnoticed, and when they do, you have a choice. Do you know internally that you did well and therefore move forward to your next action, or do you blame and get angry at those who didn't clap? Building your resiliency means you build up our inner compass of excellence and rightness and do what you feel is right, even if no one is looking.

DON'T EXPECT APPLAUSE STORY

In this video, Jennifer shares one of her key learnings from her work with Meg Wheatley.

https://bit.ly/3lYzjeS

SUSTAIN YOUR COMMITMENT, FOR THE WORK IS ON YOU

Charles Dickens said, "The best way to lengthen out our days is to walk steadily and with a purpose." There are teachers who sadly start counting down the number of days to the end of the school year on the first day of school. Countless cartoons on Facebook share the refrain, "Is it only Monday?" or "Is it Friday yet?" We must build our stamina and our resiliency to sustain ourselves when daily challenges await us. In 2020, we have collectively grown our capacity to work from a social distance and video teach remotely. We have been challenged by this type of teaching since we are humans, fortified by what we previously thought of as the only way: in-person teaching and learning. Yet with a connection to our purpose, we learned school can be done differently. Our strategies for how to get our work done have changed, but our purpose to help students achieve and grow is steadfast and endures. No doubt another challenge will be ahead of us and we need to sustain our commitment to our work so we can manage that one as well.

RECOGNIZE THAT YOU WON'T BE EVERYONE'S CUP OF TEA

I once dated a man who broke up with me because he was "used to girls with long hair who wore short skirts." I wore pants and had short hair. And that was okay. Actually, *more* than okay. It was the best breakup explanation I ever heard. I wasn't his cup of tea. And you won't be everyone's cup of tea either. The world is a big, big place. As the Dalai Lama said, "People take different roads seeking fulfillment and happiness. Just because they're not on your road doesn't mean they've gotten lost." And remember that saying from an unknown person: "There are over seven billion on earth and you're going to let one person ruin your day? Don't." Build resiliency by continually reminding yourself that our time here is short, the world is big, and life is too precious to stay unhappy for too long. There are lots of types of tea.

KEEP PERSPECTIVE, PEOPLE

There is an iconic photograph of the Milky Way with an arrow imposed on it that points to a little star and the notation, "You are here." Many of us have a tendency to not be able to look past our own belly button at times. It's understandable. In the helping professions, we are other-focused in our work—supporting students, patients, clients, and customers. Perspective is key. Martin Buber tells a story in *Tales of the Hasidim* (Schocken, 1991):

> Rabbi Simcha Bunam Bonhart of Przysucha (1765–1827) used to say, "Everyone must have two pockets, with a note in each pocket, so that he or she can reach into the one or the other, depending on the need. When feeling lowly and depressed, discouraged or disconsolate, one should reach into the right pocket, and, there, find the words: 'For my sake was the world created." But when feeling high and mighty one should reach into the left pocket and find the words: "I am but dust and ashes."

As we develop and build resiliency, we need to see the "You are here" arrow at our location in relation to the entire of the Milky Way. We need to notice there is a big world out there and gain perspective in our everyday lives so we can move forward in healthier and more evolved ways.

PERSPECTIVE, PEOPLE STORY

In this story, Jennifer shares aloud her looking at the poster of where she sits within the context of the universe and what it teaches her about perspective.

https://bit.ly/3w2nyIP

DIMENSIONS—BUILD RESILIENCY

Do sit ups for your psyche

Assess your fragility

See everything as a growth opportunity

Don't Expect Applause

Sustain Your Commitment, for the Work Is On You

Recognize That You Won't be Everyone's Cup of Tea

Keep Perspective, People

Facet #5: Build Resiliency Characteristics & Continuum			
Characteristics	**Stage 1**	**Stage 2**	**Stage 3**
Takes care of emotional and psychological hygiene as a responsibility to self and others.	I take sick days. I have a group of colleagues/family to share challenges with, and I am present when others need to share with me.	I am strategic about choosing to whom and how I express challenges. I use these moments not to complain but to seek ideas about how to speak up and be proactive. I take mental health days if I need to.	I value myself and am aware of my own emotional and mental states. I am aware of the mind-body connection. I recognize that my energy and stress are felt by the collective. I consistently check in with others. I take steps to cultivate awareness of low energy and model self and community care.
Sustains commitment and energy for the work.	I find my work purposeful and meaningful, and I often rely on others to buoy and help me sustain my energy.	I have an inner purpose for my work and am aware of my own responsibility to maintain an appropriate energy level when challenges occur.	I have strategies to maintain high energy levels for work. I have a strong community to turn to for support when work is challenging and difficult. I am invested in the work with a capital "W" and know my day-to-day responsibilities align with a greater goal and purpose.
Has boundaries; works to manage both personal and professional responsibilities.	I am aware of the tensions of balancing professional and personal life. I have started but am not consistent about putting supports in place to maintain a balance between my professional and personal lives.	I understand that life requires continually rebalancing priorities and that responsibilities change over time. Based on my needs, I consciously choose to "tip" this balance occasionally, and I am mindful and intentional about doing so. I set up scaffolds and protocols to do this effectively.	I understand the need for limits and boundaries, and I have created the structures I need to live a full life. I understand my personal needs in connection with the needs of the workplace. I adjust as needed and in response to others. I support others in living with ambiguity.

Facet #5: Build Resiliency Characteristics & Continuum			
Characteristics	**Stage 1**	**Stage 2**	**Stage 3**
Manages grief and disappointment appropriately.	I understand that anger and sadness will come into the workplace and into communications during stressful times, and that there are positive ways to manage that. I don't yet have much success in managing grief or frustration, and my emotions often interfere with my work.	I am working to become more mindful of my emotions, and I am self-regulating myself more consistently. I strive to speak and respond during times of stress and sadness in a way that doesn't leak my frustration or sadness onto others. I find productive ways to share sadness and my emotional state.	I am aware that disappointment and delight are part of work, and I work through both intentionally and with empathy. I work conscientiously to make sure my emotions don't overtake me in my communication with others. I support others without judgment when they are doing this work.
Deals with uncertainty and ambiguity in the workplace in productive and healthy ways.	I am stressed by the unknowns in work. I am aware that uncertainty is part of life, but I am not comfortable with uncertainty and I seek concrete next steps often in order to manage my anxiety.	I am becoming aware that uncertainty is constant and am okay with some ambiguity. Vagueness does not absolutely destabilize me. I have identified centering practices to use in uncertain times and have tried a few.	I understand and manage ambiguity, and I have the bandwidth to support others in doing so. I center myself each day and live more often in the middle rather than at emotional extremes. I am self-controlled and self-managed.

Build Resiliency: Self-Talk by Stages

Another way to look at the characteristics of this facet is to experience what self-talk might look like at each stage. What might you say to yourself or to others at each stage of building resiliency?

Facet #5: Build Resiliency Self-Talk by Stages			
	Stage 1	Stage 2	Stage 3
What am I saying to myself?	"I am doing some self-care, but not a lot." "I recognize that if I don't take care of myself it can affect my team, but that is challenging for me." "I notice, often too late, that I am over-committed and my level of activity causes me to be less than my best in my work and/or in my personal life."	"I am getting more consistent and aware of the need to care for myself physically, emotionally, and psychologically, but it can still be challenging." "I am becoming more attuned to my moods and they affect others. I am aware that I should interact with my colleagues professionally regardless of my feelings. I am getting better at anticipating when challenges to do this arise."	"I consistently practice physical, emotional, and psychological self-care. My self-care practices are so routine that I seldom have to think about them." "I support others attending to their self-care." "I consistently look forward and within. I am able to manage my personal and professional life so I don't get off track. I arrange for what I need to be successful and ask for what I need from my team."
What am I saying to others?	"I am learning to manage myself, my attitude, and my energy so I can be a better colleague for the work we need to do."	"I recognize the effect I may have on you, and I have started to use strategies to make sure I am having a positive effect on our team."	"I support you in your journey toward a life-work balance that supports a complete life."

Build Resiliency: Self-Assessment

Another way to look at building resiliency is by self-assessing behaviors that align with its related characteristics. What might you do or say if you were progressing through the stages of developing awareness around building resiliency? For each statement, select the response that most represents where you feel you are.

- I take care of myself physically so I can withstand the challenges of my job.
  - ☐ I haven't thought about it.
  - ☐ I have given this some thought, and I'm getting better at this.
  - ☐ I have given this a lot of thought, and I am very good at this.
- I use my personal time for non-work related activities.
  - ☐ I haven't thought about it.
  - ☐ I have given this some thought, and I'm getting better at this.
  - ☐ I have given this a lot of thought, and I am very good at this.
- I have friends and family members with whom I can talk about my work challenges. I feel supported by this group.
  - ☐ I haven't thought about it.
  - ☐ I have given this some thought, I'm getting better at this.
  - ☐ I have given this a lot of thought, and I am very good at this.

- I feel equipped to handle stressors and negative situations at work, and I respond in ways that will not be seen as overly emotional.
  - ☐ I haven't thought about it.
  - ☐ I have given this some thought, and I'm getting better at this.
  - ☐ I have given this a lot of thought, and I am very good at this.
- I continually find ways to connect to the bigger reasons my work matters.
  - ☐ I haven't thought about it.
  - ☐ I have given this some thought, and I'm getting better at this.
  - ☐ I have given this a lot of thought, and I am very good at this.
- I have worked to find ways to support myself when work becomes challenging.
  - ☐ I haven't thought about it.
  - ☐ I have given this some thought, and I'm getting better at this.
  - ☐ I have given this a lot of thought, and I am very good at this.
- I am beginning to make peace with workplace highs and lows related to my routines and responsibilities. I can anticipate them most of the time, and when I can't, I am able to stay balanced.
  - ☐ I haven't thought about it.
  - ☐ I have given this some thought, and I'm getting better at this.
  - ☐ I have given this a lot of thought, and I am very good at this.
- When I am overwhelmed at work by my moods, others' emotions, or the pace of work, I manage it quickly and efficiently.
  - ☐ I haven't thought about it.
  - ☐ I have given this some thought, and I'm getting better at this.
  - ☐ I have given this a lot of thought, and I am very good at this.
- I see new tasks and challenges as fresh and challenging rather than overwhelming. I know I can handle them.
  - ☐ I haven't thought about it.
  - ☐ I have given this some thought, and I'm getting better at this.
  - ☐ I have given this a lot of thought, and I am very good at this.
- I am aware that being disappointed and feeling negative about my work product and experiences is inevitable, and I can find solace when it happens.
  - ☐ I haven't thought about it.
  - ☐ I have given this some thought, and I'm getting better at this.
  - ☐ I have given this a lot of thought, and I am very good at this.
- I am able to cheer for others when they feel defeated or overly stressed by work.
  - ☐ I haven't thought about it.
  - ☐ I have given this some thought, and I'm getting better at this.
  - ☐ I have given this a lot of thought, and I am very good at this.

Now that you have selected your responses:

Look. Look for patterns. Where are you most aware/least aware?

Reflect. Which statements surprise you and merit future thought and attention?

Consider. How might learning more about yourself in response to these statements support your development and assist you in your work?

Build Resiliency: Exercises for Development

All of these exercises align with the parts of the continuum and the self-assessment in one way or another. There is no specific sequence for these exercises. All thinking and reflection is good.

Remember:

- These are intentionally called exercises, in contrast to activities. The goal is to develop in this facet. This type of growth doesn't always feel good or easy.
- You can decide which exercises align with your specific focus within the continuum for this facet. You can do some of the exercises—or you can do them all. Self-determination rules.
- There is no expectation that the exercises be done perfectly; there is no perfect score.
- There is no time limit on how long an exercise should take.

EXERCISE 1: Take a Deep Breath

Purpose: To learn a self-talk protocol to help you see situations with more clarity and less emotion.

Guiding Tips: If you are harassed, abused, or compromised in any way, take actions beyond completing this exercise. This exercise is helpful for when you can manage your response to a situation through a more rational internal dialogue.

Directions: The SBAR protocol (Situation, Background, Assessment, Recommendations) is a process most commonly used in hospitals for nurses to describe situations to doctors through a common protocol. It requires that you answer questions in a factual manner and might result in speeding up your ability to calm down more quickly. With a specific triggering situation, ask yourself the following questions in this order:

- **S/Situation.** What is happening? What just happened? What action took place? Describe the situation concisely and watch your use of adjectives and adverbs and consider your chosen verbs, as well. Are your word choices neutral? Do they state the facts as you saw or heard without presuming intent or motivation?

  ____

  ____

  ____

- **B/Background.** What relevant factors led to this moment? Describe the details of what led to this moment. Mention only those that are relevant.

  ____

  ____

  ____

- **A/Assessment.** What do you think is going on? What are your inferences or assumptions? They are not *the* truth. They are the "movie in your head" or the "path your brain went down" to form a hypothesis. Name them as inferences or assumptions.

  ____

  ____

  ____

- **R/Recommendations.** What do you recommend that you do next? What actions might be helpful now? What actions might not be good? What is the simplest thing to do? What is the fastest thing to do? Would those choices benefit you now as well as tomorrow and/or several days from now?

  ____

  ____

  ____

Post-Exercise Reflection:

- What did I notice about the problem as I initially stated it?
- As I went through the SBAR process, what changes did I notice in myself and my thinking?
- How might this protocol be useful to me in the future?
- How might this protocol support me in building my resiliency?

EXERCISE 2: Thanks for Nothing

Purpose: To learn to see the good in challenging and painful memories and to see the good in all experiences. A friend once said to me after I told her about an emotionally painful interaction with a colleague, "Wow. Send that woman a thank-you note. You will know how to not get into that situation again." This exercise asks you to think about your painful moments and to be thankful for those from whom you learned boundaries and the need for explicit communication.

Guiding Tips: This exercise or reframing isn't always possible or the right thing to do. You must feel safe and distanced from the event enough to learn from the experience. This may help you view the situation differently. Remember, this is truly a thank-you note. It isn't to vent or write sarcastically with a vindictive intent. There are many learning opportunities in painful moments. Consider this thank-you note as a maturity marker where you are able see beyond the initial pain to the possible benefits.

Directions: Think of a bad experience you've had: You didn't get the job you wanted. You felt wounded by someone's comment at a meeting. You didn't set expectations clearly and had additional work to do as a result. If you were to thank a person involved for what *didn't* go right, what would your thank-you note say? Use this scaffold.

Dear ______________,

Looking back at _________ (difficult moment), I want to thank you.

You _________ (what they specifically did or did not do in the moment) and _________ (say more if needed).

As a result, the experience left me (knowing/doing/better understanding) _________.

As a result of that moment and your actions, I was better able to _________, and I ended up _________.

Thank you again for _________.

In gratitude,

____

Post-Exercise Reflection:

- What insights do I have from writing this thank-you note?
- How might I use this reframing exercise for other moments in my past?

EXERCISE 3: Talking to Your Saboteurs/Adversaries

Purpose: To become more aware of the inner voices that sometimes sabotage you. Thinking about these voices in a fun way can externalize them as common to everyone and help you relate to them more productively.

Guiding Tips: Don't worry about picking the "right" voice for this exercise. Recognize that most of us, if not all of us, hear internal adversaries and manage or don't manage them well. You are learning to acknowledge and not be overly affected by your inner voices.

Directions: Choose the internal adversary that trips you up most often. If you can't decide between one, two, or even three voices, try this exercise with each one. These saboteurs are based on saboteurs mentioned in the book *Positive Intelligence: Why Only 20% of Teams and Individuals Achieve Their True Potential and How You Can Achieve Yours* by Shirzad Chamine (Greenleaf Book Press, 2012).

Types of Internal Adversary Voices:

The Judge: The inner voice that constantly finds fault in you, others, circumstances, and conditions.

The Avoider: The inner voice that asks you to avoid difficult and unpleasant tasks and conflicts.

The Controller: The inner voice that needs to take charge, control situations, and bend people's actions to your will.

The Hyper-Achiever: The inner voice that asks you to depend on constant performance and achievement for self-respect and self-validation.

The Hyper-Rationalizer: The inner voice that focuses on processing everything rationally, including relationships. This inner voice makes you impatient with people's emotions and has you regard emotions as unworthy of time or consideration.

The Pleaser: The inner voice that compels you to try to gain acceptance and affection by constantly helping, pleasing, or rescuing.

The Stickler: The inner voice that feels the need for perfection, order, and organization.

The Restless: The inner voice that is constantly searching for more excitement through a new activity or perpetual busyness.

The Victim: The inner voice that wants you to feel emotional and temperamental to get attention and affection.

Once you have picked one inner voice to focus on, start a dialogue. Ask questions.

- What is their name? (What do they like to be called?)

  ____

  ____

- When were they born? (Within your life, when did they crop up or join in with more frequency?)

  ____

  ____

- What do they want from you? (In the most generous interpretation of their behaviors, what are they protecting you from?)

  ____

  ____

- What could you do to make them go away sooner, more often, in specific situations? (Do you need to say something to them? Take an action?)

  ____

  ____

Post-Exercise Reflection:

- How did it feel to look at this adversary's voice as separate from the rest of you?
- When might this be a good exercise to do again (i.e., at which moments might this externalization be helpful)?

EXERCISE 4: Learning to be Optimistic

Purpose: To reframe situations in a more optimistic way using the process from *Learned Optimism: How to Change Your Mind and Your Life* (Vintage, 2006) designed by the University of Pennsylvania psychologist Martin Seligman. While you can't control your experiences, you can control your explanations. Reframing situations optimistically will build your resiliency muscles over time.

Guiding Tips: Reframe your experience within a few hours of a situation or experience rather than waiting several days.

Directions: In a moment of disappointment when things didn't go well, you didn't get the answer you were hoping for, or an event wasn't as successful as you wanted it to be, reframe the event by recognizing that the results are not personal, pervasive, or permanent. Right after the challenging moment, ask yourself:

1. How is this not personal? How might this be not about me as a person or as a human being of worth? How might I see this event as external from me?
2. How can I localize this experience to a given moment and not have it ooze into my personal life? How can I avoid turning this into the feeling of a pervasive failure in all aspects of my life?
3. How can I recognize that this moment is short-term and not see it as a static, permanent state? Can I envision that a similar future experience could be different? What in my sphere of control in this situation might I be able to change for a future event?

Post-Exercise Reflection:

- In what moments do I believe this reframe would be most helpful?
- How does it feel to frame an experience using this perspective?

EXERCISE 5: There Is Sadness Again

Purpose: To learn self-compassion and to distance yourself from overwhelming emotions. This externalization technique was featured in a talk by Meg Wheatley for the Warriors for the Human Spirit cohort.

Guiding Tips: You may have to speak your selection aloud as many as ten times or more. Don't stop too soon or you might not feel the benefit you could if you continued the repetition.

Directions: When you start to feel a strong emotion—anger, sadness, grief, loss, disappointment, shame, embarrassment—threaten to take over your ability to think clearly and remain centered, address the emotion out loud in the third person.

> "There is Sadness."
>
> "There is Loss."
>
> "There is Anger."

Repeat the words out loud. You don't need to yell to feel the effect. See if, with extended repetition, the feeling inside you lessens.

Post-Exercise Reflection:

- Did I feel the strength of my emotion lessen by using this practice?
- Did the length of time I felt the emotion shorten?
- Did I have a greater sense of compassion for myself as a result of externalizing the emotion?
- Through externalizing an emotion, might I begin to regard it as something that all people experience at some time? (i.e., Sadness isn't something I alone feel.)
- Did externalizing the emotion help me feel stronger and more resilient?

EXERCISE 6: Yeah, Nah Boundary Setting

Purpose: To build up linguistic skill to effectively set boundaries.

Guiding Tips: Modify the directions to suit your own context and linguistic style. Be sure to respect community/workplace context and be authentic and true to yourself.

Directions: When asked to do something that you would prefer not to do, cannot do, or won't do, use this scaffold to affirm your boundary and script your "No."

1. Be gracious. Begin with an acknowledgment. For example, "Although this work is important," or "I know I agreed."
2. Be simple and direct and share your "no" in only one or two sentences. "Although this work is important to me, I need to decline your request to volunteer to join the committee. I need to honor my family's needs" or "I know I agreed to meet you tomorrow, but after reviewing my schedule, I now realize that I won't be able to give it my best attention at that time. Could we reschedule?"
3. Do not defend, debate, or over-explain your feelings. That demeans yourself and gets in the way of your next step, which is to move forward with your decision.
4. When you are faced with resistance, repeat your statement or request one more time. Keep your tone neutral to avoid escalating the situation.
5. Hold firm. If you give in and agree, or if you overly apologize for holding your boundary, you ignore your own needs and invite others to do so, as well.

Post-Exercise Reflection:

- How did I feel during the experience?
- How do I feel about the outcome afterward?
- How does setting boundaries help me become more resilient and healthier?

EXERCISE 7: Quote Journaling

Purpose: To learn what others have said about the importance of resiliency and to find support from others' words.

Guiding Tips: There is no one right quote to choose for this exercise. Pick the one that resonates most for you at this time.

Directions: Look through the quotes. Choose one. Take five to ten minutes to answer the questions about the quote you chose. Why did you choose this quote? What connections are you making between the quote and your ideas around resiliency? What actions does this quote inspire you to take to build your resiliency?

- "Breathe deeply and know that who you are can withstand the experience of conflict that living requires."—Mark Nepo, American author
- "The greater the force of your compassion, the greater your resiliency in confronting hardships."—Dalai Lama, the highest spiritual leader of Tibet
- "Success is not final, failure is not fatal: it is the courage to continue that counts." —Winston Churchill, former prime minister of the United Kingdom
- "Although the world is full of suffering, it is also full of the overcoming of it." —Helen Keller, American author and political activist
- "Adversity has the effect of eliciting talents which in prosperous circumstances would have lain dormant."—Horace, Roman poet
- "Inner resiliency and the ability to bounce back are personal qualities... Align yourself with someone who has this kind of resiliency so that your own can be strengthened. Find another oak to weather the storm with you. Anyone who is in touch with his or her core self will always respond." —Deepak Chopra, American author and alternative-medicine advocate.
- "It is not the strongest of the species that survive, nor the most intelligent, but the one most responsive to change."—Leon C. Megginson, misquoting Charles Darwin
- "All shall be well, and all shall be well, and all manner of thing shall be well." —Julian of Norwich, English anchorite of the Middle Ages
- "Even the darkest night will end and the sun will rise."—Victor Hugo, French author
- "The whole world is a narrow bridge; the important thing is not to be afraid." —Rabbi Nachman of Bratslav, founder of the Breslov Hasidic movement in Judaism
- "This is your world. Shape it or someone else will."—Gary Lew, adjunct lecturer at the University of California, Davis
- "And the day came when the risk to remain tight in a bud was more painful than the risk it took to blossom."—Elizabeth Appell, American poet
- "I must be a mermaid... I have no fear of depths and a great fear of shallow living."—Anaïs Nin, American writer
- "When you're ready to quit, remember why you started."—Unknown

- "It ain't over till it's over."—Yogi Berra, Coach, manager, American baseball great
- "Let everyone sweep in front of his own door, and the whole world will be clean."—Johann Wolfgang von Goethe, German writer
- "Things are not always right because they are hard, but if they are right one must not mind if they are also hard."—Winston Churchill, former prime minister of the United Kingdom
- "Caring for myself is not self-indulgence, it is self-preservation." —Audre Lorde, American author and political activist

____

____

____

____

____

____

Post-Exercise Reflection:

- In what ways did this exercise increase my confidence in my own resiliency?
- What might I do next to continue to embody this attitude and possible newfound strength?

EXERCISE 8: Interviewing an Inspirational Other

Purpose: To interview someone who inspires you with their strength and resiliency.

Guiding Tips: The age of the person you interview doesn't matter. The person might have an academic role in which they have studied resiliency or have lived experience managing personal or professional challenges. Choose someone you anticipate is able to self-reflect and articulate how they built their own resiliency and is willing to share their personal and professional journey (obstacles and celebrations, joys and disappointments) with you.

Directions: Seek out an individual you believe has intentionally grown their resiliency. Set up thirty to forty-five minutes to ask about what rough patches, disappointments, or challenging situations they've faced, what they did to move through those, how they bounced back, what they learned, and what they do now to stay strong. Write a thank-you note to your interviewee about how you were affected by what you learned.

Possible interview questions:

- When you look back on your professional life (and personal life, if they are comfortable sharing), what are some moments of disappointment or pain that built your resiliency? What happened? What did you do in the moment? What did you learn?
- As you continue this work, what do you do to stay strong?

- What structures and supports do you have in your life that help you physically manage challenges that come your way? (Examples: exercise, healthy eating, etc.)
- What tactics do you use in challenging moments? Do you use a breathing, meditation, or quieting practice?
- How do you cultivate relationships in your life outside of work? (Examples: family, partner, pets, friends)
- Do you intentionally work on building a growth mindset and work on your learning edges? If so, in what ways and in which situations?
- Do you use a self-talk practice that helps you stay optimistic?
- Do you have a coach or someone who works with you to help you consider your assumptions and belief systems?
- Do you have a compassion practice (self-compassion, loving kindness)?
- What do you do ground yourself or center yourself and gain greater perspective on your life and your work? Do you watch TED talks, go to spiritual centers, read, listen to podcasts?
- What is your plan to build your resiliency and develop yourself and your skill sets? Do you go to conferences, mastermind groups, take online courses, join professional learning communities, follow reading lists?
- What suggestions do you have for me to build resiliency?

One of the greatest gifts is that of being good at disappointment: having non-persecutory, speedy, resilient, emotional digestion.

–Alain de Botton, British author and founder of The School of Life

Post-Exercise Reflection:

- What were my key takeaways from this interview?
- What did I learn about myself by interviewing this individual?
- In what situations have I been reluctant to explore the kind of ideas addressed here?
- What might I need to unlearn?
- What will it look like to see progress in embodying a new learning or understanding?

Chapter Reflection Questions: Build Resiliency

- What might I add to my self-care strategies?
- What energy do I absorb from others? How can I recognize and discharge negative energy?
- What energy do I radiate most often?
- In what areas am I most fragile, i.e., not the best at taking care of myself?
- What can I tell myself in order to shift my mindset during challenges to turn them into learning moments?
- Do I know what motivates me?
- What methods do I use to regain my perspective and balance myself?

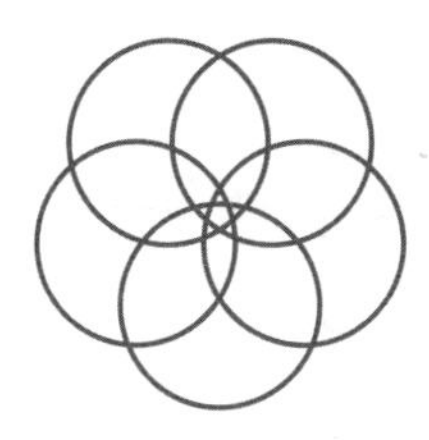

CHAPTER SIX
What's Next? Going Inward, Upward, Outward, Onward

Everything will change. The only question is growing up or decaying.
—Nikki Giovanni, American poet

KNOW Your Identity
SUSPEND Certainty
BUILD Resiliency
TAKE Responsibility
ENGAGE in Reciprocity

Guiding Questions

- What do I know now?
- What do I now know that I don't know?
- Which ideas had I never thought about?
- What excites me to learn next?
- In what ways do I see stretching a learning edge affecting my work?
- What areas have I noticed could benefit from further reflection?

As you finish this text and the exercises and contemplations found within, here are a few ideas, reminders, and pieces of encouragement as you move forward and continue to stretch at your edges.

What's Next? Going Inward, Upward, Outward, Onward: Dimensions

KEEP A BEGINNER'S MIND

There is a possibility one may start to feel overwhelmed by the immensity of the task ahead. It may feel as though there is too much to do, to learn, or to "get right." Stay in a beginner's mind. This phrase comes from the book *Zen Mind, Beginner's Mind: Informal Talks on Zen Meditation and Practice* by Zen teacher Shunryū Suzuki. Suzuki notes that "in the beginner's mind there are many possibilities; in the expert's mind there are few." Remember that you cannot learn unless you "empty your cup." In other words, be a constant work in progress. Live within the awareness that there is always more to learn. We aren't just proving ourselves, but instead always improving ourselves. There is no right way to do this work nor a need to rush to the finish line. Stay available. Stay open. No one knows the right answer. The only wrong answer is not to take the journey at all.

ANTICIPATE FALLBACK

Reverting to habitual ways of doing things is to be expected. Behaviors deeply embedded in our being and our common ways of working are easier and more comfortable than stretching and developing new ways of behaving. Stasis is easier. And in times of crisis, stress, or pressure, we often devolve. In times of pain, we go into survival mode. Don't beat yourself up. Instead, when you notice it, try to move forward again to stretch at your learning edges and become a bigger self.

KNOW YOU ARE NOT ALONE

Pushing ourselves to mature and develop requires walking a path that not all choose. Not everyone who grows old grows up. Evolving requires risk, loss, and disappointment—and also results in greater meaning, joy, and strength. Not everyone will understand you. Many of us struggle to move beyond group think—what others agree to in order not to make waves. Some will not join you on this path. And as you are on this path you also need to know you are not alone. There are those who are with you, stretching their learning edges, asking themselves "What else?" Others are on the journey with you.

SEE THE INTERCONNECTEDNESS

These five facets do not exist in siloes, unrelated and separate from one another. They are not a collection of divided parts of a self, but instead is a system of skills, capabilities, and capacities that are inextricably interconnected. The way you were raised and your identities connect with your ability to suspend certainty. Your skills and mindsets about engaging in reciprocity and taking responsibility for your language in meetings is coupled with your sense of resiliency. The Venn diagram that begins every chapter shows how the facets are interlaced and the web of skills connect all together. Development in one facet can lead to development in another. The facets are complementary and connected to each other. Developing capacity in all the facets allows individuals and their teams to be able to adapt more successfully. Research on collective efficacy, relational trust, self-efficacy, and adult development speaks to the importance of development to organizations' productivity, achievement,

> *For it is important that awake people be awake... the darkness around us is deep.*
>
> –From *A Ritual to Read to Each Other* by William Stafford

occupational wellbeing, and organizational health. Developing within these five facets allows individuals and teams to change gears and shift direction and to move in a new way that benefits the organization as a whole.

This book asks you to look *inward,* stretch yourself *upward* developmentally, and take new actions *outward* to more effectively support your work on teams. These final exercises are to help you move *onward*—thinking past yourself as an individual to what learning-edge work might do at a team level.

What's Next? Exercises for Development

EXERCISE 1: Agreements and Belief Statements—A Reflective Conversation

Communications consultant Stewart Levine created a team generativity assessment for the American Society for Training in which he asked teams to reflect and consider where they were in terms of skill level in a variety of important attributes. The adapted team agreement below describes a set of aptitudes related to the five facets in this text and asks team members to agree to a way of working and developing together specifically around the five facets in this book.

Directions: Use the following belief statements and ask yourself individually: To what degree do I take these actions? On a scale from one to five with five being "always" and one being "never," where do I fall? Then redo the activity asking yourself as a team member or asking the team as a group: To what degree do I think we as a team take these actions? On a scale from one to five with five being "always" and one being "never," where do we fall?

From the assessment, you can individually determine where you might want to stretch next, or after a calibrating discussion with your team, you can determine in which areas the team might move from its current state to a more highly effective and healthy state.

Agreement for Increasing Development Around the Five Facets	INDIVIDUAL How do I rank?	TEAM How do WE rank as a team?
	NEVER ——► ALWAYS	NEVER ——► ALWAYS
Know Your Identity		
I/We believe in the importance of self-awareness and provide time and opportunities to study ourselves.	1 2 3 4 5	1 2 3 4 5
I/We build our skill set to become more other-aware, striving to see the bigger picture from the balcony.	1 2 3 4 5	1 2 3 4 5
I/We know that we each have different ways of looking at the world, and we pose questions to learn different perspectives.	1 2 3 4 5	1 2 3 4 5
I/We commit to being compassionately curious about others.	1 2 3 4 5	1 2 3 4 5

Agreement for Increasing Development Around the Five Facets	INDIVIDUAL How do I rank?					TEAM How do WE rank as a team?				
	NEVER ⟶ ALWAYS					NEVER ⟶ ALWAYS				
Suspend Certainty										
I/We value humility, recognizing that we don't know everything.	1	2	3	4	5	1	2	3	4	5
I/We work to see not just "either/or" but "both/and," not just black and white, but shades of gray.	1	2	3	4	5	1	2	3	4	5
I/We work on the quality of our inquiry, making sure that we are compassionately curious, thoughtful, and respectful.	1	2	3	4	5	1	2	3	4	5
I/We step into conversations with an open mind, willing to be educated.	1	2	3	4	5	1	2	3	4	5
I/We believe that when members see things differently, our first question should be, "What can we learn and teach each other about our different perspectives?".	1	2	3	4	5	1	2	3	4	5
Take Responsibility										
I/We take collective responsibility to build our skills in collaboration.	1	2	3	4	5	1	2	3	4	5
I/We take collective responsibility to contribute to resolving conflict in humane and growth-producing ways.	1	2	3	4	5	1	2	3	4	5
I/We understand how critical it is to have clarifying and difficult conversations quickly.	1	2	3	4	5	1	2	3	4	5
I/We take responsibility for having difficult conversations with ourselves, our supervisors, our teammates, and others.	1	2	3	4	5	1	2	3	4	5
I/We spend time making sure we all understand the task at hand when we begin a new initiative or project, and we align ourselves not just to the letter of the work but to the spirit of it.	1	2	3	4	5	1	2	3	4	5
Engage in Reciprocity										
I/We are committed to a high level of respect and caring for all members.	1	2	3	4	5	1	2	3	4	5
I/We hold a mindset of appreciation and concern for others' well-being.	1	2	3	4	5	1	2	3	4	5
Build Resiliency										
I/We are proactive in our work to become less compromised and less fragmented.	1	2	3	4	5	1	2	3	4	5
I/We work on our collective resiliency in order to support one another with more graciousness.	1	2	3	4	5	1	2	3	4	5
I/We work on sitting with discomfort, disappointment, and dissonance so we are less swept along with the status quo.	1	2	3	4	5	1	2	3	4	5
I/We look at our work more intentionally and healthfully.	1	2	3	4	5	1	2	3	4	5
I/We take care of ourselves and each other during challenging times so we can live up to our remarkable potential.	1	2	3	4	5	1	2	3	4	5

EXERCISE #2: A Letter from Your More Stretched Self

Write a letter from your future more stretched self at your edges—your more developed self. What might your more developed self wish your current self to know about you in a few years? What might they share with you? What do they want to remind you of that you have forgotten? What is less overwhelming now that it is known? What can you now see more clearly? How are you acting more wisely? And what did this hard but important work teach you that you integrated into the person you are further down the road? What inspiration does your future self have for your current self as you begin this journey?

EXERCISE #3: A Visual of Your Stretch Marks

Make an annotated visual that marks your learning edges and your stretch marks.

Possible ideas: Several bridges, doors, lenses, or a map with a curved road annotated with stretch marks—perhaps one per facet. Or before and after "photos", or a collage of images that show your key learnings from each of the five facets and markers showing where you are and where you are headed. You might annotate your visual with symbols or words that have meaning for you.

EXERCISE #4: Venn the Diagram

Use the book's cover visual with the rings connecting all five facets as your base image. Then, through symbols or pictures, dotted lines, arrows, or whatever representation you choose, capture the interconnectedness of the five facets and how you see the facets integrating with each other beyond the rings.

- Example: Know Your Identity and Build Resiliency blur when learning about anti-oppression practices and systemic racism. The Venn occurs when Know Your Identity (biases, limitations, and assumptions) blends into Build Resiliency (the ability to manage uncertainty and disappointment).
- Example: Engage in Reciprocity and Take Responsibility come together when working on curriculum design for your grade level. The Venn occurs when Engage in Reciprocity (treat others with respect and dignity) and Take Responsibility (express concerns, not complaints).
- Example: Suspending Certainty, Take Responsibility, and Know Your Identity blend when leading a team through analyzing data. The Venn occurs when the task requires you to Suspend Certainty (remain open to different points of view), Know Your Identity (knowing your preferred work style), and Take Responsibility (express your requests in productive ways).

You might pick common group tasks and see how they Venn the facets when done most successfully. Tasks such as:

- Communicating with families;
- Writing evaluations;
- Co-teaching;
- Participating in an IEP;
- Facilitating a staff meeting;
- Collaborating with colleagues.

Determine how the facets Venn with each other in those moments and how each of the facets impacts your ability to work collaboratively in those situations.

In the end, work with these exercises is only a start of the exploration with this material. The developmental work this book asks you to undertake in real time is important, and if done consistently, can offer a greater range of ways to successfully engage in teams and contribute to the shared purpose of educating students. The development and stretch asked for is quite aspirational and at times is terribly impractical. It isn't for the fainthearted or the passive. It is work for the adventurous and the committed. Although there are so many who "want the answer," there is no "right" way to stretch at your learning edges. Peter Block, management consultant and author, wrote a book titled *The Answer to How Is Yes: Acting on What Matters.* The question, "How do I do this right?" he says, is often "a defense against action. It is a leap past the question of purpose, past the question of intentions, and past the drama of responsibility." He writes, "Transformation comes more from pursuing profound questions than seeking practical answers." The five facets in this book ask for more than answers. The book accompanies you on your developmental journey but doesn't offer you a complete map. Spanish poet Antonio Machado wrote, *"Caminante, no hay camino, se hace camino al andar,"* which translates to: "Wanderer, there is no path. The path is made by walking." We will never get there unless we say yes to our own development and unless we take our next step and stretch ourselves to move forward and to grow (up) at work.

See you on the path.

> *Maturity beckons... asking us to be larger, more fluid, more elemental, less cornered, less unilateral, a living conversational intuition between the inherited story, the one we are privileged to inhabit and the one, if we are large enough and broad enough, moveable enough and even here enough, just, astonishingly, about to occur.*
>
> —"Maturity" in *Consolations: The Solace, Nourishment and Underlying Meaning of Everyday Words* by David Whyte

> *Uncover what is keeping you from taking action. In most instances, it's not that you can't do something. You choose not to because the price is higher than you want to pay. By owning your choices, you take responsibility for your decisions.*
>
> —Shane Parrish, "Yes, It's All Your Fault: Active and Passive Mindsets," Farnam Street

"[T]here is nothing, believe me, more satisfying, more gratifying than true adulthood. The adulthood that is the span of life before you. The process of becoming one is not inevitable. Its achievement is a difficult beauty, an intensely hard won glory, which commercial forces and cultural vapidity should not be permitted to deprive you of.

You are your own stories and therefore free to imagine and experience what it means to be human without wealth. What it feels like to be human without domination over others, without reckless arrogance, without fear of others unlike you, without rotating, rehearsing and reinventing the hatreds you learned in the sandbox. And although you don't have complete control over the narrative (no author does, I can tell you), you could nevertheless create it."

—Toni Morrison, Wellesley College commencement, 2004

What's Next: Reflection Questions

- What is still alive for me as I finish this book?
- What crossroads have I reached?
- What has been worthy of my time?
- What has my attention now? What matters to me now?
- What do I know now that will help me reconstruct or interrupt the narrative of my current work?
- What means the most to me or was of greatest value in this book?
- What flame do I want to carry into my future interactions?
- In what situations do I want to declare, "This is what I want to do next," as I move forward with my learning journey?
- What strikes me as most important to share? To discuss further? To reflect on by myself? To reflect on with others?
- What conversations can I have that will bring something new into the world?

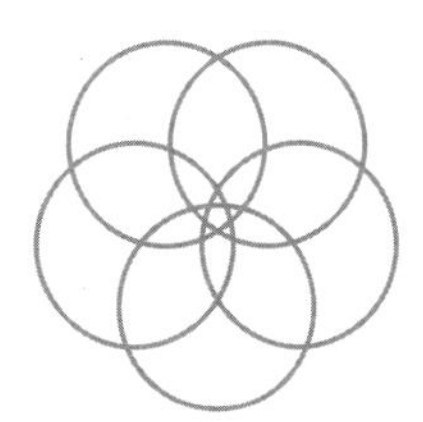

Works Cited, References & Resources

Abrams, Jennifer and Valerie Von Frank. *The Multigenerational Workplace: Communicate, Collaborate, and Create Community.* Corwin Press, 2013.

Abrams, Jennifer. *Hard Conversations Unpacked: The Whos, the Whens, and the What-Ifs.* Corwin Press, 2016.

Abrams, Jennifer. *Having Hard Conversations.* Corwin Press, 2009.

Abrams, Jennifer. *Swimming in the Deep End: Four Foundational Skills for Leading Successful School Initiatives.* Solution Tree Press, 2018.

Achi, Zafer. "Never Has There Been a Better Time for Development in Action." *Cultivating Leadership*, 27 Mar. 2020, www.cultivatingleadership.com/leadership/2020/03/never-has-there-been-a-better-time-for-development-in-action.

Aguilar, Elena. *Onward: Cultivating Emotional Resiliency in Educators.* Jossey-Bass, 2018.

Aguilar, Elena. *The Art of Coaching Teams: Building Resilient Communities That Transform Schools.* Jossey-Bass, 2016.

Aguilar, Elena. *The Art of Coaching: Effective Strategies for School Transformation.* Jossey-Bass, 2013.

https://theantioppressionnetwork.com/allyship/

The Arbinger Institute. *Leadership and Self-Deception: Getting Out of the Box.* Berrett-Koehler, 2010.

Arrien, Angeles. *The Four-Fold Way: Walking the Paths of the Warrior, Teacher, Healer, and Visionary.* Harper Collins, 1993.

Arrien, Angeles. *The Second Half of Life: Opening the Eight Gates of Wisdom.* Sounds True, 2007.

Benjamin, Ben E., et al. *Conversation Transformation: Recognize and Overcome the 6 Most Destructive Communication Patterns.* McGraw-Hill, 2012.

Benson, Jeffrey. *Hanging In: Strategies for Teaching the Students Who Challenge Us Most.* ASCD, 2014.

Berger, Jennifer Garvey. *Changing on the Job: Developing Leaders for a Complex World.* Stanford University Press, 2012.

Bernstein, Elizabeth. "Worried About a Difficult Conversation? Here's Advice From a Hostage Negotiator." *The Wall Street Journal,* Dow Jones & Company, 14 June 2020, www.wsj.com/articles/worried-about-a-difficult-conversation-heres-advice-from-a-hostage-negotiator-11592139600.

Block, Peter. *Community: The Structure of Belonging.* Berrett-Koehler, 2009.

Block, Peter. *Stewardship: Choosing Service Over Self-Interest.* Berrett-Koehler, 2013.

Block, Peter. *The Answer to How Is Yes: Acting on What Matters.* Berrett-Koehler, 2003.

Bregman, Peter. "13 Ways We Justify, Rationalize, or Ignore Negative Feedback." *Harvard Business Review,* 14 Feb. 2019, hbr.org/2019/02/13-ways-we-justify-rationalize-or-ignore-negative-feedback.

Bridges, William. *Transitions: Making Sense of Life's Changes.* Da Capo Press, 2004.

Briskin, Alan, Sheryl Erickson, Tom Callanan, and John Ott. *The Power of Collective Wisdom: And the Trap of Collective Folly.* Berrett-Koehler, 2009.

Brown Brené. *Braving the Wilderness: The Quest for True Belonging and the Courage to Stand Alone.* Random House, 2017.

Bryk, Anthony S., and Barbara Schneider. *Trust in Schools: A Core Resource for Improvement.* Russell Sage Foundation, 2004.

Buber, Martin. *Tales of the Hasidim (The Early Masters/The Later Masters).* Schocken Books, 1991.

Bucks, Garrett. "I Actually Don't Know How to Be in Community with Others." *The White Pages,* August 3, 2020. https://thewhitepages.substack.com/p/i-actually-dont-know-how-to-be-in?utm_medium=email&utm_campaign=cta

Carroll, Lewis. *Alice's Adventures in Wonderland.* MacMillan, 1865.

"The Center for Compassion and Altruism Research and Education (CCARE)." *The Center for Compassion and Altruism Research and Education,* 2019, ccare.stanford.edu.

Chamine, Shirzad. *Positive Intelligence: Why Only 20% of Teams and Individuals Achieve Their True Potential and How You Can Achieve Yours.* Greenleaf Book Group Press, 2012.

The Choices Program, Brown University, www.choices.edu

Clark, Timothy R. *The 4 Stages of Psychological Safety: Defining the Path to Inclusion and Innovation.* Berrett-Koehler, 2020.

Costa, Arthur L., and Bena Kallick, editors. *Learning and Leading with Habits of Mind: 16 Essential Characteristics for Success.* Association for Supervision and Curriculum Development, 2018.

Costa, Arthur L., and Robert J. Garmston. *Cognitive Coaching: A Foundation for Renaissance Schools.* 2nd ed., Christopher-Gordon Publishers, 2002.

Cuddy, Amy. *Presence: Bringing Your Boldest Self to Your Biggest Challenges.* Little, Brown & Company, 2015.

DeWitt, Peter M. *Collaborative Leadership: Six Influences That Matter Most.* Corwin Press, 2017.

Donohoo, Jenni, and Steven Katz. *Quality Implementation: Leveraging Collective Efficacy to Make "What Works" Actually Work.* Corwin Press, 2019.

Donohoo, Jenni. *Collective Efficacy: How Educators' Beliefs Impact Student Learning.* Corwin Press, 2017.

Dooley, Scott, et al. "Design Thinking Bootleg." *Stanford d.school, Stanford d. school,* 30 Apr. 2020, dschool.stanford.edu/resources/design-thinking-bootleg.

Drago-Severson, Eleanor, and Jessica Blum-DeStefano. *Leading Change Together: Developing Educator Capacity Within Schools and Systems.* ASCD, 2018.

Drago-Severson, Eleanor, and Jessica Blum-DeStefano. *Tell Me So I Can Hear You: A Developmental Approach to Feedback for Educators.* Harvard Education Press, 2016.

Dweck, Carol. Mindset: *The New Psychology of Success.* Ballantine Books, 2007.

Edmondson, Amy C. *Teaming: How Organizations Learn, Innovate, and Compete in the Knowledge Economy.* Jossey-Bass Pfeiffer, 2014.

Edmondson, Amy C. *The Fearless Organization: Creating Psychological Safety in the Workplace for Learning, Innovation, and Growth.* John Wiley & Sons, 2019.

Emel, Bobbi. *The Bounce Blog,* 2020, www.thebounceblog.com.

Fernandez-Armesto. *Humankind: A Brief History.* Oxford University Press, 2004, p. 170.

Freedman, Michael. "David L. Bradford: How Do You Manage Up in the Workplace?" *Insights by Stanford Business*, 8 Oct. 2013, www.gsb.stanford.edu/insights/david-l-bradford-how-do-you-manage-workplace.

Fullan, Michael. *Nuance: Why Some Leaders Succeed and Others Fail.* Corwin, 2018.

Gall, Sharon Nelson-Le. "Help-Seeking Behavior in Learning," *Sage Journal Review of Research in Education,* Vol. 12, Issue 1. Chapter 2, January 1, 1985, pp. 55-90.

Garmston, Robert J., and Bruce M. Wellman. *The Adaptive School: A Sourcebook for Developing Collaborative Groups.* Christopher-Gordon Publishers, 1999.

Garmston, Robert J., and Diane P. Zimmerman. *Lemons to Lemonade: Resolving Problems in Meetings, Workshops, and PLCs.* Corwin Press, 2013.

Godin, Seth. *What to Do When It's Your Turn (And It's Always Your Turn).* The Domino Project, 2013.

Gottman, John, et al. *Eight Dates: Essential Conversations for a Lifetime of Love.* Workman Publishing, 2018.

Goulston, Mark. "Don't Get Defensive: Communication Tips for the Vigilant." *Harvard Business Review Blog Network,* 2013, blogs.hbr.org/2013/11/dont-get-defensive-communication-tips-for¬the-vigilant.

Goulston, Mark. *Talking to "Crazy": How to Deal with the Irrational and Impossible People in Your Life.* American Management Association, 2016.

Grant, Adam M. *Give and Take: Why Helping Others Drives Our Success.* Penguin Books, 2014.

Haidt, Jonathan. *The Righteous Mind: Why Good People Are Divided by Politics and Religion.* Pantheon Books, 2012.

Hammond, Zaretta. *Culturally Responsive Teaching and The Brain: Promoting Authentic Engagement and Rigor Among Culturally and Linguistically Diverse Students.* Corwin Press, 2015.

Hargreaves, Andy, and Michael Fullan. *Professional Capital: Transforming Teaching in Every School.* Teachers College Press, 2012.

Hargreaves, Andy, and Michael T. O'Connor. *Collaborative Professionalism: When Teaching Together Means Learning for All.* Corwin Press, 2018.

Heath, Chip, and Dan Heath. *Decisive: How to Make Better Choices in Life and Work.* Crown Business, 2013.

Heath, Chip, and Dan Heath. *Switch: How to Change Things When Change Is Hard.* Crown Business, 2010.

Heifetz, Ronald A., et al. *The Practice of Adaptive Leadership: Tools and Tactics for Changing Your Organization and the World.* Harvard Business Press, 2009.

Hirschman, Albert O. *The Rhetoric of Reaction: Perversity, Futility, Jeopardy.* Belknap Press, 1991.

Hofstede, Geert, et al. *Cultures and Organizations: Software of the Mind.* McGraw-Hill, 2010.

Hollis, James. *Finding Meaning in the Second Half of Life: How to Finally, Really Grow Up.* Avery, 2006.

Hurwitz, Sarah. *Here All Along: Finding Meaning, Spirituality, and a Deeper Connection to Life--in Judaism (After Finally Choosing to Look There).* Spiegel & Grau, 2019.

Intercultural Development Inventory. https://idiinventory.com/

Kaufman, Scott Barry. *Transcend: The New Science of Self-Actualization.* Tarcher-Perigee, 2020.

Kegan, Robert, and Lisa Laskow Lahey. *How the Way We Talk Can Change the Way We Work: Seven Languages for Transformation*. Jossey-Bass, 2001.

Kegan, Robert, and Lisa Laskow Lahey. *Immunity to Change: How to Overcome It and Unlock the Potential in Yourself and Your Organization*. Harvard Business Review Press, 2009.

Kegan, Robert, et al. *An Everyone Culture: Becoming a Deliberately Developmental Organization*. Harvard Business Review Press, 2016.

Kegan, Robert. *In Over Our Heads: The Mental Demands of Modern Life*. Harvard University Press, 2003.

Kegan, Robert. *The Evolving Self: Problem and Process in Human Development*. Harvard University Press, 2001.

Killion, Joellen. *The Feedback Process: Transforming Feedback for Professional Learning*. Learning Forward, 2015.

Kim, Daniel H. *Introduction to Systems Thinking*. Pegasus Communications, 1999.

Kise, Jane A. G. *Unleashing the Positive Power of Differences: Polarity Thinking in Our Schools*. Corwin Press, 2013.

Kohlberg, Lawrence. *The Psychology of Moral Development: The Nature and Validity of Moral Stages*. Harper & Row, 1984.

Lambert, Linda, et al. *Liberating Leadership Capacity: Pathways to Educational Wisdom*. Teachers College Press, 2016.

LaPorte, Danielle. *The Desire Map: A Guide to Creating Goals with Soul*. Sounds True, 2014.

Lazare, Aaron. *On Apology*. Oxford University Press, 2015.

Lerner, Harriet. *The Dance of Connection: How to Talk to Someone When You're Mad, Hurt, Scared, Frustrated, Insulted, or Desperate*. Harper Collins, 2001.

Lerner, Harriet. *The Dance of Fear: Rising above Anxiety, Fear, and Shame to Be Your Best and Bravest Self*. Harper Collins, 2004.

Lerner, Harriet. *Why Won't You Apologize?: Healing Big Betrayals and Everyday Hurts*. Touchstone Press, 2017.

Levine, Stewart. *The Book of Agreement: 10 Essential Elements for Getting the Results You Want*. Berrett-Koehler, 2002.

Lieberman, Matthew D. *Social: Why Our Brains Are Wired to Connect*. Crown Publishers, 2013.

Lipton, Laura, and Bruce M. Wellman. *Learning-Focused Supervision: Developing Professional Expertise in Standards-Driven Systems*. MiraVia, 2013.

Lorde, Audre. *Sister Outsider: Essays and Speeches*. Crossing Press Feminist Series, 2007.

Markus, Hazel Rose, and Alana Conner. *Clash! 8 Cultural Conflicts That Make Us Who We Are*. Hudson Street Press, 2013.

Marshak, Robert J. *Covert Processes at Work: Managing the Five Hidden Dimensions of Organizational Change*. Berrett-Koehler, 2006.

Maslow, A. H. "A Theory of Human Motivation." *Psychological Review*, vol. 50, no. 4, 1943, pp. 370–396., doi:10.1037/h0054346.

McDonald, Joseph P., et al. *The Power of Protocols: An Educator's Guide to Better Practice (The Series on School Reform)*. Teachers College Press, 2013.

McLaren, Karla. *The Language of Emotions: What Your Feelings Are Trying to Tell You*. Sounds True, 2010.

McLeod, Saul. "Abnormal Psychology." *Simply Psychology,* 5 Aug. 2018, www.simplypsychology.org/abnormal-psychology.html.

McLeod, Saul. "Nature vs. Nurture in Psychology." *Simply Psychology,* 20 Dec. 2018, www.simplypsychology.org/naturevsnurture.html.

Meyer, Erin. *The Culture Map: Breaking Through the Invisible Boundaries of Global Business.* Public Affairs, 2014.

Mogel, Wendy. *The Blessings of a Skinned Knee: Using Jewish Teachings to Raise Self-Resilient Children.* The Penguin Group, 2001.

Molinsky, Andy. *Global Dexterity: How to Adapt Your Behavior Across Cultures without Losing Yourself in the Process.* Harvard Business Review Press, 2013.

Neff, Kristin. *Self-Compassion: The Proven Power of Being Kind to Yourself.* William Morrow Publishers, 2012.

Newkirk, Thomas. *Embarrassment: And the Emotional Underlife of Learning.* Heinemann, 2017.

Newport, Cal. Deep *Work: Rules for Focused Success in a Distracted World.* Grand Central Publishing, 2016.

O'Hara, Maureen, and Graham Leicester. *Dancing at the Edge: Competence, Culture and Organization in the 21st Century.* International Futures Forum, 2012.

Palmer, Parker J. *The Courage to Teach: Exploring the Inner Landscape of a Teacher's Life.* Jossey-Bass, 1998.

Parrish, Shane. "Timeless Insight for Business and Life." *Farnam Street,* 2020, fs.blog.

Parrish, Shane. "Yes, It's All Your Fault: Active vs. Passive Mindsets." *Farnam Street,* 18 Mar. 2019, fs.blog/2019/03/active-mindset/.

Platt, Alexander D., et al. *The Skillful Leader: Confronting Mediocre Teaching.* Ready About Press, 2000.

Plett, Heather. *The Art of Holding Space: A Practice of Love, Liberation and Leadership,* Page Two, 2020.

Porter, Susan Eva. *Relating to Adolescents: Educators in a Teenage World.* Rowman & Littlefield Education, 2009.

Rock, David. *Your Brain at Work: Strategies for Overcoming Distraction, Regaining Focus, and Working Smarter All Day Long.* Harper Business, 2009.

Salzberg, Sharon. *Real Happiness at Work: Meditations for Accomplishment, Achievement, and Peace.* Workman Press, 2014.

Sandberg, Sheryl. *Lean in: Women, Work, and the Will to Lead.* Alfred A. Knopf, 2013.

Schein, Edgar H. *Humble Inquiry: The Gentle Art of Asking Instead of Telling.* Berrett-Koehler, 2013.

The School of Life. *The School of Life: An Emotional Education.* The School of Life Press, 2019.

"The Science of a Meaningful Life." *Greater Good,* greatergood.berkeley.edu.

Seligman, Martin E.P. *Learned Optimism: How to Change Your Mind and Your Life.* Vintage Books, 2012.

Senge, Peter M., et al. *Schools That Learn: A Fifth Discipline Fieldbook for Educators, Parents, and Everyone Who Cares About Education.* Crown Business, 2012.

Sheridan, Richard. *Joy, Inc.: How We Built a Workplace People Love.* Penguin, 2015.

Slap, Stan. *Bury My Heart at Conference Room B: The Unbeatable Impact of Truly Committed Managers.* Penguin, 2010.

Slap, Stan. *Under the Hood: Fire up and Fine-Tune Your Employee Culture.* Penguin, 2015.

Steele, Dorothy M., and Becki Cohn-Vargas. *Identity Safe Classrooms: Places to Belong and Learn.* Corwin Press, 2013.

Stone, Douglas, and Sheila Heen. *Thanks for the Feedback: The Science and Art of Receiving Feedback Well.* Penguin Books, 2014.

Suzuki, Shunryū. *Zen Mind, Beginner's Mind: Informal Talks on Zen Meditation and Practice.* 50th Anniversary Edition, Shambhala Publications, 2020.

Sweeney, Linda Booth. *When a Butterfly Sneezes: A Guide for Helping Kids Explore Interconnections in Our World through Favorite Stories.* Pegasus Communications, 2001.

Taylor, Barbara Brown. *Holy Envy: Finding God in the Faith of Others.* New York: Harper One, 2019, p. 49.

Thorp, Tris. *Feeling Stuck? Check Your Baggage.* Chopra, October 18, 2017. https://www.chopra.com/articles/feeling-stuck-check-your-baggage.

Waack, Sebastian. "Collective Teacher Efficacy (CTE) According to John Hattie." *Visible Learning,* 12 Oct. 2018, visible-learning.org/2018/03/collective-teacher-efficacy-hattie/.

Waldschmidt, Daniel E. *Edgy Conversations: How Ordinary People Can Achieve Outrageous Success.* Hydra Publishing, 2014.

Wheatley, Margaret J. *Perseverance.* Berrett-Koehler, 2010.

Wheatley, Margaret J. *So Far From Home: Lost and Found in Our Brave New World.* Berrett-Koehler, 2012.

Wheatley, Margaret J. *Who Do We Choose to Be?: Facing Reality, Claiming Leadership, Restoring Sanity.* Berrett-Koehler, 2017.

Whitman, Walt. "Song of Myself." *Leaves of Grass.* D. McKay, 1891-92, pp. 25-86.

Whyte, David. *Consolations: The Solace, Nourishment and Underlying Meaning of Everyday Words.* Many Rivers Press, 2016.

Wilkerson, Isabel. *Caste: The Origins of Our Discontents.* Random House, 2020

Wiseman, Liz, et al. *The Multiplier Effect: Tapping the Genius Inside Our Schools.* Corwin Press, 2013.

Wiseman, Rosalind. "Dealing with Grown-Up 'Mean Girls.'" *The New York Times,* Dec. 5, 2019.

www.yourmorals.org.

Zimmerman, Diane P., et al. *Transforming Teamwork: Cultivating Collaborative Cultures.* Corwin Press, 2019.

Zoller, Kendall, and Claudette Landry. *The Choreography of Presenting: The 7 Essential Abilities of Effective Presenters.* Corwin, 2010.

Index

A

B

C

D

E

F

G

H

I

J

K

W

Y

About

The Road To Learning

mira (L.)[MIR-â]: wonderful/amazing via (L.)[VE-â]: way or road

In 1596, the German astronomer Fabricus saw a third magnitude star in the constellation Cetus, the Whale. As they continued to observe it over the next century, astronomers became aware of its unusual fluctuations, now brighter, now fading, and honored it with the name Mira, the Wonderful.

As a partnership dedicated to continued development for professionals, we connect the constancy of presence and fluctuating brightness with the learning process. We believe that learning means working through the temporary dullness of not knowing, while pursuing the brilliance of new understanding. Our name, and our philosophy, combines this wonder of learning, Mira, with Via, or the road. Our publications, products, and seminars offer pathways to professional insight and growth.